ABOUT**DESIGN**

Allworth Press books may be purchased in bulk at
special discounts for sales promotion, corporate gifts,
fund-raising, or educational purposes. Special editions
can also be created to specifications. For details,
contact the Special Sales Department, Allworth Press,
307 West 36th Street, 11th Floor, New York, NY 10018
or info@skyhorsepublishing.com.

22 21 20 19 18   5 4 3 2 1

Published by Allworth Press, an imprint of Skyhorse
Publishing, Inc., 307 West 36th Street, 11th Floor,
New York, NY 10018. Allworth Press® is a registered
trademark of Skyhorse Publishing, Inc.®, a Delaware
corporation.

WWW.ALLWORTH.COM

COVER + TEXT DESIGN
Kelly Salchow MacArthur

AUTHOR PHOTOGRAPH
Michael Kroeger

TYPEFACE
Whitney, designed by Tobias Frere-Jones

LIBRARY OF CONGRESS CATALOGING-IN-PUBLICATION DATA
NAMES: Salchow, Gordon R., author.
TITLE: About design : insights + provocations for graphic
    design enthusiasts / Gordon R. Salchow.
DESCRIPTION: New York : Allworth Press, 2018. | Includes index.
IDENTIFIERS: LCCN 2017049216 (print) |
    LCCN 2017050007 (ebook) |
    ISBN 9781621536550 (e-book) |
    ISBN 9781621536543 (pbk. : alk. paper)
SUBJECTS: LCSH: Graphic arts.
CLASSIFICATION: LCC NC997 (ebook) | LCC NC997 .S16
    2018 (print) | DDC 740--dc23
LC record available at https://lccn.loc.gov/2017049216

PRINT ISBN 978-1-62153-654-3
EBOOK ISBN 978-1-62153-655-0

Printed in China

gordon salchow

ABOUT DESIGN

INSIGHTS + PROVOCATIONS
FOR GRAPHIC DESIGN ENTHUSIASTS

ALLWORTH PRESS
NEW YORK

CONTENTS

1

ABOUT**DESIGN**

FOREWORD

Like raising a child or running a restaurant, teaching is something that a lot of people think is a lot easier than it really is. Every student who has sat in a classroom begins to develop a theory about what makes a good teacher. But, inevitably, this theory reflects only the student's point of view. What it ignores is the unique dynamic that takes hold the moment a class begins.

——

When I was in design school, I sometimes imagined what would happen if one day I was asked to teach. I knew exactly how I'd be: warm, accessible, friendly, encouraging—not given to stern critiques, but instead a fountain of constructive advice, delivered in the gentle voice of an ally or collaborator rather than an authority figure. My classes would be fun. I'd be more like a friend than a teacher, really.

——

In other words, I wanted to be exactly the opposite of the best teacher I ever had, Gordon Salchow.

I entered the University of Cincinnati's College of Design, Architecture, and Art in the fall of 1975. First-year students were required to declare their concentrations upon admission. Mine was graphic design. So in the fall quarter, barely three months from my high school graduation, I was plunged into rigorous foundation studies: drawing, color, simple typography exercises. I was eager to please. My teachers were demanding. Some were nice. Some were eccentric. But I liked them all, I worked hard for their approval, and I got it. But awaiting us all was the real test: a teacher we would meet in our sophomore year.

Gordon Salchow had arrived in Cincinnati to head the department of graphic design eight years before I got there. That may as well have been a lifetime to me as a freshman; perhaps it seemed that way to him as well. Over that period of time, he had made a program that met his own exacting standards, introducing rigor, intensity, and worldliness to a place that still bore the traces of a provincial vocational school. We had seen him in the halls, expressionless, sometimes holding an unlit cigar, or oddly, a can of TaB® diet soda. At department gatherings, he would materialize, deliver a few oracular remarks, and disappear. We didn't know much about him, but we were scared of him nonetheless. At least I was. He would teach our core second-year design class, Visual Aesthetics.

Rumors about Salchow began to circulate in whispers among my classmates. He gave cryptic assignments that were sphinxlike in their inscrutability. He said things in critique sessions that made students burst into tears. He lived in a featureless white box. (As is often the case, most of these rumors had some roots in truth: the Salchow house, for instance, while not exactly a box, was by far the most modern structure in its Clifton neighborhood. And students did cry in his critiques. In my experience, a few cry in any good critique.)

On the first day of class, we were talking excitedly in the studio. Then silence fell over the room: Gordon Salchow had arrived. He briefly described his goals for the class, which probably wouldn't seem esoteric to me today; at the time, I remember listening in hushed and mystified awe. Then he explained something we hadn't heard. He was taking a sabbatical after the first quarter. So his goal would be to compress a year's worth of teaching into three months, a series of exercises that would culminate in a single project: The Cube.

I can't remember, forty years later, precisely how Salchow described this assignment. What I do remember is my sense of complete confusion. The object was to build a cube, 12-inches square on each side and then . . . what? Transform it, somehow, through the application of form and color. Somehow. Many of our assignments up to that point had been abstract, but I was always able to figure out what the professor wanted and faithfully deliver it. In this case, I didn't have a clue. If you're eager to please, there's only one thing worse than not knowing the answer: not understanding the question.

Now, I realize this was exactly the point. With a feeling of helplessness, I began my work. There were no rules, no guides, no answers. There was just the simple world of a six-sided form and my own imagination. Add a color here, take one way there. Change a straight line to a curve, a triangle to a circle, move things around and then back again, hour after hour. There was no solution to discover, just the task of building my powers of observation, attending to detail, and mastering the elements of my craft. Through it all, Salchow seemed to guide me and the rest of the class without giving away a single trick. It was the hardest and most pleasurable work I had ever done. I was a different designer when I finished.

———

It would be a long time before I understood the lessons of this class. And when I was invited to teach twenty years later, my assignments were the opposite: hardheaded, explicit, leaving nothing to doubt. I couldn't bear to subject my students to the discomfort of ambiguity, remembering how unpleasant I had found it myself. In the classroom, I was the friendliest of mentors, an easygoing coach, eager—as usual—to please. What hard work it is to be a good teacher! And, as I eventually realized, what a bad teacher I was.

———

It's remarkable how different people can interpret the same thing in different ways. One of my favorite dramatic devices, one that I never tire of in movies or in books, is the revelatory shift to a new point of view. You see a series of events transpire through the eyes of one person, and then you see the same events through the eyes of another.

———

This book is like that. Sitting in his classroom, worrying about what he'd say about my work, and then wondering what he meant by what he did say, I was too obsessed with my own fortunes to imagine that Gordon Salchow had an inner life of his own. But he did, and it is on display in the following pages. You see the world of teaching through his eyes. To a large degree, it is his highly developed self-awareness that made him such an effective teacher. It is remarkable to relive these formative moments of my own life through another person's experience.

Precise, thoughtful, and serious, Gordon did the hard work. He made each of us understand that we were important to him. When I graduated in 1980, it seemed he had been teaching forever. He would go on to teach for another thirty years.

"Assignments can be too complicated but never too simple," he writes. Reading that, I thought of my struggles with The Cube, that seemingly simple problem that changed my life. And I was reminded of something I learned from another mentor, my first boss after I graduated, Massimo Vignelli, who once described the difference between complication and complexity. A love affair that's complex is wonderful, he said, but a love affair that's complicated is a disaster.

Gordon Salchow has had a lifelong love affair with teaching. His devotion has been simple. The results have been complex. I am grateful to have been his student and even more grateful that he has given us—his former students and his students yet to come—this book. Thank you, Gordon.

Michael Bierut

ABOUT**DESIGN**

ACKNOWLEDGMENTS

I imagine that I have always seemed more stern than I feel internally. My self-diagnosis is that seriousness became my demeanor in order to camouflage some insecurity that was caused by my first thirty years as an increasingly obese young guy. At the age of thirty I designed my own extreme diet of only one small meal per day (usually a salad or a frozen TV dinner) and I lost 130 pounds in nine months. I have maintained my weight with exercise and willpower, but my chubby, somewhat solemn youth created a mindset of introspective determination. Fortunately, this helped me to realize the potential of transforming problems (including design obstacles) into achievements and nourishing a self-induced confidence. In fact, given my particular upbringing, I believe I would have had a less rewarding career and life if I had been the neighborhood stud. My early persona molded me to succeed and to ultimately cherish my adult health, family, abilities, friends, preferences, and environment. Problems can be unveiled for certain opportunities that they inherently encompass.

———

Some students may have thought that I was too harsh, but actually, I believe that I am abnormally sensitive to others' feelings because of experiencing derision from my peers during my pudgy youth. This causes me to be extra thorough and as informative in my (hopefully constructive) criticism as possible while exaggerating objectivity and sublimating my personal feelings. I also realize that this effort to be educationally comprehensive can be misconstrued as verbosity but I never wanted to shortchange or misdirect any student. Often, in fact, explaining the most important concepts extensively, or in a variety of ways, as occasionally occurs in this text, is necessary in order to effectively connect with diverse personalities.

———

I began formal design study in 1957, professional practice shortly thereafter, and teaching in 1965. My perspectives are the result of the various readings, lectures, projects, people, debates, and ideas that I have encountered. These have all blended and been edited by the prism of my own professional and educational initiatives. Singular sources for the various pieces of information or theories that are contained in this memoir cannot, consequently, be easily credited, but I must recognize the dominant influence of Rob Roy Kelly when I was his undergraduate student at the Minneapolis College of Art and Design and later while working with him at the Kansas City Art Institute. I am grateful for the superior education and inspiration that I received from others at MCAD, KCAI, and as a graduate student at Yale University, where I gained various insights through my exposure to several design pioneers, including Alvin Eisenman, Alexi Brodovitch, Herbert Matter, Walker Evans, Bradbury Thompson, Norman Ives, and others, particularly Paul Rand.

——

I most value the enriching and enjoyable decades with my constructively feisty and astute colleagues at the University of Cincinnati. I have certainly grown through the interactions with my students. I was fortunate to have well-intentioned parents. I am particularly thankful for the magical balance that has been contributed by two terrific people, my daughters Kelly and Raegen, but no one has been more important to my emotional and intellectual vigor than the most creative person I know, Kathy, whom I was smart enough to marry in 1967. Therefore, this book is dedicated to Kathy, Kelly, and Raegen. Also, I pray for ongoing creativity, health, happiness, and love concerning my engaging grandchildren (Oskar, Gable, Sutton, and Sloane). As a bonus, I appreciate my son-in-laws (James and Morgan) who are bright and kind gentlemen.

———

I appreciate the kind "Foreword" and "Afterword" contributions by Michael Bierut and Katherine McCoy. They are esteemed peers who have graciously contributed thoughtful bookends for this text.

———

I owe an additional nod of appreciation to one of my talented and industrious former students, Jesse Reed, who first read this manuscript and championed its publication.

———

This text has fewer visuals than is the norm for a book that concerns art and design because I hope that, in this way, it will serve to inspire perpetually individualized visual investigations and exponential knowledge by the readers. Also, I feel that our graphic design profession has matured to the point where sans-image texts, although concerning our visual world, can be appreciated, much as I fantasized the world when enthralled by radio dramas in my youth.

—

We can now easily exploit the Internet to research and access historical, editorial, and visual references. This eliminates the need for me to reproduce a bunch of accumulated examples, and I can also choose not to automatically incorporate a traditional glossary or a bibliography. Hopefully, my editorial regurgitations herein are worthy and tantalizing enough to beg for elaboration in other sources beyond this text.

—

The large type sizing is done not simply as a favor to readers of my generation, since I hope that every age-group will check it out, but to exaggerate some of my primary points and even allow for efficient—and hopefully enticing—skimming if one is so inclined.

PREFACE

Designers analyze existences in order to conceive and to create improved manifestations. *Graphic designers* plan and produce in a rational and an interesting way in order to promote communication.

Graphic designs may inform, persuade, beautify, direct, identify, clarify, or entertain. Design helpfully transforms commonalities while contributing to and thereby documenting our civilization.

Innovative design additionally elevates the human spirit and serves to reveal new insights and intrigue while occasionally birthing significant creative artistry.

We live in a visually compelling world where everyone is a player. Everybody makes daily design decisions through their purchases of objects and clothing, furniture arrangements, organization of editorial copy, and in the production of documents for bosses, clients, or the government. There are everyday, often automatic decisions concerning communications, purchases, and our environment. Everyone exercises their opinions about and even produces design. Ideally, aspects of this book will help all readers to be able to better appreciate, select, or make design-related decisions. I hope that its content is clear enough to assist amateurs. Aspiring designers should consult as many such sources as possible. For the most experienced, this material may add an alternative way to analyze what is encountered and to create, or it might clarify an individual's own points of view. In particular, I believe that chapters 1, 3, and 5 could be illuminating for any adult concerning our visual world. Additionally, chapters 2 and 4 are perhaps a bit more targeted toward design/art students and educators.

—

My approach is occasionally unique—maybe even original—and sometimes assertive, but it is grounded in some humble but long-term experiences and thoughtful objectivity. Much of what follows reflects simple common sense, sometimes so obvious that it has not been previously documented or described.

———

I can make a sandwich but I'm not a chef; I can play an accordion but I'm not a musician. However, many graphic design greenhorns unabashedly inflate their preparedness or authority.

———

Anyone who has reasonable smarts along with some basic skills can drive an automobile, care for simple injuries, or play a sport, but there are vast differences between the skills of a novice and those of professionals. I have now been driving for six decades. I began with some structured lessons and I then passed the licensing tests. My current traffic instincts developed as the result of thousands of hours behind the wheel while focusing on that activity with a decent degree of concentration. This combination of training and experience provides a level of safety for others and gives me some instinctual confidence. I know that I am a better driver now than I was as a teenager, but I would not survive on a competitive racetrack. Indeed, in most fields, the more that we know about some activity as avowed amateurs, the more we are likely to appreciate the accomplishments of our heroes.

———

Conversely, in the visual arts, aside from some college art/ design majors, instruction often tends to be superficial, biased, or purely subjective. We are asked to copy pictures, use the proper color within the lines, or to simply "express." Often, art class is a therapeutic respite between studious work on other topics. Even in some schools dedicated to the creative and performing arts, the visual arts lessons are less rigorous and often supportive of the performing events (doing the posters or painting the stage sets for high school plays). Children are expected to simply make art while their parallel interest in music is rewarded with serious lessons and hours of practice before they are asked to compose or even perform complete works. If we aspire to competitive athletics, instruction, conditioning, and drills become a dedicated and pragmatic way of life. Visual acuity is at least as complex but also as teachable as is driving, piano playing, or soccer. It includes inspired subjectivity but it also incorporates a ton of objective knowledge and many elusive intellectual, visual, and motor skills.

People favor familiar designs even though such preferences have usually been formed by a tattered fabric of accidental lifetime encounters (i.e., traditional-looking furniture pieces that are often tacky imitations, copycat buildings, and mundane pictures) as opposed to open-minded study. Also,

there is so much design junk around us that it causes a kind of ugliness fatigue to set in, making us immune to such environmental grime and the derivative violations.

Everyone designs. Amateurs and professionals, as well as the occasional geniuses, create our visually digested world. Most design is casual, and much of it is imposed on us without our being able to select the most enriching pieces. Condescending graphics infest our mailboxes. We are daily forced to encounter constructed buildings and monuments. Self-serving organizations impose clumsy objects, like sidewalk publication dispensers or funky vacation knickknacks, on our psyche. We are so inundated with this vomit that our conscious minds become numbed to its existence while our subconscious absorbs it. We are bombarded by visual swill that goes unnoticed while parallel noises and stink offend us. It is ironic, consequently, that some people so easily interpret the lack of knowledge and skill in visual art as exemplifying primitive charm while clumsiness in any other form of human endeavor (dance, basketball, politics, etc.) is unlikely to be forgiven. Parallel to this is the common assumption that skillfully realistic imagery reflects creativity, although we realize that skilled mechanics are not likely to be inventive engineers, nor are crossword puzzle whizzes consequently equipped to craft romantic poems.

A situation becomes high art/design only if proficiencies, theoretical underpinnings, and creative instincts are manifested, along with purpose, while permeating the viewer's soul. Most Western citizens have not grown up amid a pattern of environmental orientation, information, and education concerning design that parallels our growth in other fields. Our musical tastes progress because we evolve from simple jingles through more and more elegant arrangements. We selectively expose ourselves to works that are formed by the most accomplished musicians. Similarly, we gradually move from mother's milk to alternative tastes and end up considerately choosing which foods are preferred and what restaurants to support.

As parents we will attend any number of junior swim meets, but we also have strong feelings about the athletic strengths and weaknesses of our favorite professional teams. If they're not playing at a superior level, we know it and will likely resist endorsing them with our ticket investments. Olympians in many unheralded sports spend four gut-wrenching years training and sacrificing to have the ability to compete during one captivating week. We individually prefer a certain sport, one ethnic food over others, and a type of music, but we have encountered, respect, and know quite a bit about the alternatives in each category. We usually experience healthy portions of some variety before exercising the notion of individual taste. The public's visual naïveté is mirrored by an inconsistent quality of education in art/design even at the college level, where the studio courses are often not as information driven, skills intensive, or focused on critical seeing and thinking as those in almost any other field.

——

Individual taste is not the thing that determines whether a design is good or bad. We are not born with the "gift" of good taste or mature artistry any more than we are born with the "gift" of automatic musicianship or basketball prowess. We do not hold equal credentials for doing and judging design quality just because most of us are sighted from birth or because we "know what we like."

I believe that all of us have a share of latent talent and that everyone certainly has the need to participate—but just like all other activities, education and practice greatly enhance one's abilities and the credibility of one's judgments.

After pluralistic knowledge and skills have been soaked up, meaningful spontaneity is possible and it becomes legitimate. It took many lessons and awkward practices before I was comfortable with a proper service motion for tennis. Now I serve spontaneously (although some opponents suggest that it's still quirky). An experienced tennis player reacts without thought but is supported by years of preparatory information and training. There is no chance of experiencing "the zone" if Joe Shmoe has not paid some sweaty dues, no matter how "naturally gifted."

Eventually, a few people in any field are able to add their own magic to a foundation of knowledge and skills by producing work that excels.

I appreciate superior athletes and recognize my parallel shortcomings, partly because of my own time and efforts on tennis courts. It is interesting that, in most endeavors, what we identify as "acceptable" is simple to achieve, while "good" is just OK and "great" looks, but is anything but, simple.

I will mostly use common terms, but some terminology may be inappropriate or misleading because we have occasionally developed popular definitions that contradict the original intentions, or because given words that may be broadly applicable are too closely associated with one aspect of design. Consequently, a few unique terms and explanations will surface in this document.

There are always latent concepts and previously undiscovered but helpful viewpoints that can contribute to our dialogue. In fact, common beliefs provide the basis for and an encouragement of examination and elaboration or alteration rather than automatic repeating. I believe that my particular engagements have provided me the opportunity to formulate a few fresh insights. So while I do not intend or claim to be revolutionary, my text is sometimes cheeky and will occasionally introduce some virgin ways to consider and clarify design principles and methodologies. Students of my forty-five years as a design educator have tested and employed these ever-evolving initiatives while I have continuously examined and adjusted their validity and use. At the least, I hope to add to the already rich existing art/ design conversation. Conversely, I acknowledge that the lion's share of this content is based on many long-established tenets that have provided the shoulders for my subsequent perspectives to stand on.

———

This content admittedly leans toward *graphic* design, but I believe that much of it has parallel validity for considerations inherent to other design and visual art disciplines. We share in the reliance on form and aesthetics as our foundation.

FORM

+

2

INTRODUCTION

I will use the word "form"
as an inclusive identification
for a succinct set of
visual elements:
point,
line,
shape,
space, and
color.

I believe this element list is logical and complete, although I respect that others may favor a slightly different mix. Incidentally, the word "form" should not be confused with my subsequent definition of the word "shape." Form is not a singular thing or a simple preliminary agenda, but the umbrella term for everything that is seen. It is something that is tangible, and since I am emphasizing graphic design, our primary concern is for *visual form.* **_Visual form_ is something—an existence—that we can see.** We see rather than smell or taste color, lines, pictures, etc. Even when we see nothing, perhaps gazing into the night sky, we are visually perceiving nothingness. Empty or "negative" space is something—an existence that can be visually perceived.

—

Additionally, visual form is a conveyor of (and causes) messages, ideas, and feelings. Red does not float out there without informing us that it is a particular red. That is its initial message. A red flower suggests something different than a red puddle, and it may innately cause a personalized sensation. Such factors introduce additional layers of communication. Seeing red may make you feel hot or anxious, or it might trigger delight because it reminds you of your first bicycle or a valentine greeting.

—

Everything that we see transmits information to us and inspires certain actions, thoughts, or feelings.

This is true for all colors and everything else (points, lines, shapes, spaces, pictures, symbols, letterforms, environments, objects, etc.) that is viewed. Some of these visual statements are interpreted in a similar way by a majority of viewers, while other aspects of the message may be understood differently by different cultures, professions, or individuals. A designer should consider the constants as well as the variables. Blue likely triggers a different feeling for an airline pilot than it does for a police officer or a psychologist. Every viewer innocently interprets through a personally subjective filter. For this reason, designers must reduce misinterpretations by seeking to be as diligently objective as possible. We should attempt *purpose* in every *form* ingredient. Even then, the designer's own uniqueness will be irrepressibly incorporated. However, any shared ambiguities are part of what injects some joie de vivre.

How something communicates greatly influences *what* is communicated. The designer, knowingly or innocently, always adds his or her voice (inflection/ accent/dialect/translation/pronunciation) to the content through his or her manipulation of form. We cannot be absolutely neutral or bury our own voice. Each person, approaching the same objective, will produce something different. Designing requires insight, objectivity, and clarity, but the designer's personal voice also humanizes the result, making it more approachable. An accomplished actor is able to give alternative meanings to a standard line of dialogue, depending on inflection, volume, etc. A musician can produce any number of different interpretations with the same score. So too does the designer manage and enhance or shroud a message. Again, how we say something is often more impactful than the words that are uttered. Imagine screaming with a huge black image in the middle of a page as opposed to whispering with a tiny yellow version of the same image down in a corner. Beyond this functionality wish, *high design* **adds inspirational delight to a creation (flowering when the solution is original, illuminating, alluring, and effective). This is when creativity, art, and design merge.**

Visual form is the graphic designer's primary vehicle for communication and

expression. I must note, however, that it is virtually impossible to isolate one sense from the others within our daily experiences. Our seen stimuli are consistently reinforced or altered by concurrent odors, sounds, tastes, or touches. Multiple senses contribute to every individual perception, but in design we must be particularly cognizant of and in control of the visual factors because those are our primary career tools.

—

Musicians communicate and express primarily through sound, writers through words, and chefs through taste, smell, sight, and touch (perhaps such multiplicity, along with experiential transience, makes high artistry even more elusive in cuisine than for those of us who can mostly concentrate on one sense). In terms of design, **every**

thing and every aspect of that thing that we see is a message, a piece of information, an insight, or a nuance that either contributes to, skews, or detracts from an overall agenda. A particular bright orange versus a washed-out color, a sensuous curve instead of an awkward bend, the center location on a format or crowding to an edge, the way a line ends (sharply cut off or rounded). All such occurrences are message choices that, to varying extents, are appropriate or inappropriate for a given situation.

If we parallel literature with the visual language, the bigger messages (such as the choice of green as opposed to purple) might be akin to a phrase; the darkness or intensity of that green is like an individual word; how much green may be likened to the spellings. Superior authors choose words, considering phrasing and structure very carefully. If a word is misspelled there is distraction, and if a word is misplaced the meaning may be altered. Likewise, if many words are misused, the story is mangled. In an ideal design, every individual thing that we see (what, where, how much, etc.) is appropriately employed by the designer to eliminate visual static. Even a little dirt is annoying, subconsciously if not consciously. Unfortunately, we have been numbed into overlooking the prevailing missteps that exist in our visual environment. Genuine masterpieces, in any artistic field, have no aesthetic static as they engage our emotional core. Although some people profess that perfection is always unattainable, **artistic mastery** (visual, musical, editorial, etc.) **may be the only home for unbounded flawlessness.** An elevated level of control requires initially studious thought, practice, and patience while the protagonist's knowledge, pure insights, skills, and core sensibilities are assimilated. A commingled expertise can eventually be spontaneously expelled without conscious thought after it becomes second nature. This is when instincts become useful, one's freedom surfaces, and epiphanies may bloom. We then discover whether that artist/designer additionally has a rare, singular gift that will separate him or her from the tribe. Legitimate freedom depends on preparation.

I should introduce the idea of ***visual reality*** as opposed to physical reality. Visual reality is a truism and requires that the designer employ visual objectivity while not assuming that another measurement (such as mathematical) is more valid. For instance, a measured square may not be a visual square depending on the shape of the context or what else exists within that square. A common color example of this interactive phenomenon is that a small gray shape will be noticeably darker in a white environment than it will be when seen side by side with its physical duplicate in a black environment.

There are naysayers concerning rational thought in art and design. They may misrepresent the notion of free expression by suggesting that visual objectivity dampens the magic of artistic creativity. Poetry is certainly a high art form, but poets choose each word very precisely while crafting their often sparse sentences. Musicians are only equipped to create freely once they have the tools and the savvy as the result of countless lessons and endless practice. While I acknowledge that there may be occasional self-taught savants, for most people a methodical studiousness is necessary as a prerequisite for visual artistry and for genius to perform. When we have the knowledge substructure and an appropriate set of skills, plus some confidence, we are then able to freely create, explore, express, and maybe break new ground by challenging some customs and common assumptions.

—

Visual artistry is a particularly difficult world to understand since knowledge, skill, and practice are often devalued in favor of that mystical born-with-a-gift exaggeration. Also, our eyes are constantly bombarded with visual calories, and this innocently leads the masses to assume some authority. A common boast is, "I know what I like and so you cannot tell me what is good." We all tend to initially favor traditional pictures, architecture, and furniture that emulates what we became familiar with as children, whether or not new options have substantive pizzazz.

—

Details are mighty. If a person has not

been adequately introduced to alternatives or to the value of details, an educated preference cannot be exercised. The differences between a significant mid-century modernist chair and the knockoffs are in the finely tuned proportions, materials, and crafting, along with some enigmatic evidence of the creator. These combine to imbue it with a mysteriously appreciable dignity.

—

Most citizens are not schooled to discern good design from bad in the way that they have didactically learned other subjects. We very selectively progress from mushy foods to more diverse palates, from simple lullabies to performances that require serious financial and time investments. Because of our developed understanding, we notice if a dancer stumbles or if a quarterback fumbles or if an auto exhaust fouls the air, but we tend to ignore

much of the visual stench in our environment.

We are able to approach most things with relative sophistication because of sequential progressions involving a series of objective experiences, lessons, and judgments. The consumer seems more willing to encounter a new performer than a cutting-edge design, and we are better equipped to judge the aforementioned.

—

People value the beauty of pure sound in musical compositions without needing lyrics while they ridicule the parallel of non-representational imagery

("a monkey could do that"). This is a bit ironic since it has been discovered that people gravitate toward the innate proportions, patterns, colors, etc. that appear in nature but seem to be uncomfortably judgmental when encountering these naked qualities in "abstract" art.

———

In this context, I cannot resist an audacious suggestion that our common terminology of "realism" (representational) or "abstraction" is backward. Abstract art is actually what is seen (color, line, shape, etc.) so it is, if you will, realistic. Realistic (representational, figurative) art is an abstraction of something else that is not really seen. A picture of a tree is an abstraction of a tree, but it is really green, etc. I will defer to the common usage and adopt the flawed popular definitions.

———

Kelly (my designer/daughter) has incorporated a smattering of simple visuals in this chapter to reinforce some of the concepts.

POINT

.

A *point* is an identifiably specific spot or location.
I will not dwell on this category because, despite their
omnipresence, *points* tend to be the simplest and most
inconspicuous of all of the visual elements. However, they
may be too easily ignored because of their abundance and
diminutiveness. *Points* are produced
in a variety of ways, so they
crowd our seen environments
and should be orchestrated
to appropriately contribute
within every design.

The period that ends my previous sentence is an obvious *point* message, but so are the corners of this page, the endings of the *lines*, the ends of each of the letterforms being read. *Points* occur where lines crisscross or abruptly connect to each other or even where ingredients almost touch one another.

———

The center of a seemingly empty page is a *point* that may not be noticed until something else exists on that page. We all see when an addition is not centered, which means that we are suddenly seeing it in relation to the preexisting center *point*.

———

There are two types of *point*. A *point* may be explicit or implicit. An explicit *point* communicates a precise, visible place as the result of a mark. An implicit *point* may be less specifically legible or defined unless attention is directed to it, but it still exists as a specific location. These two types are additionally explored in my examination of the element category of *line*.

———

This is a convenient place to interject that there is an implied viewing situation or distance for most images and this should be taken into account. When driving on the highway, distant objects are *points*, as are the stars in our sky. As we approach, they may become *shapes*. The primary viewing circumstance is a factor to consider when designing. Some graphic design situations are highly controllable in terms of what is perceived, such as for a handheld item. If your eyesight would allow very very close viewing of these periods, they might transform into *shapes* (with *color*).

———

A mass of *points* may additionally communicate an implied *shape* or a series of *points* may suggest an implied *line*. . . . . This reveals another nuance of form manipulation and perception. That previously mentioned center of a page may be interpreted as an implied *point* unless it is made explicit. There are a number of ways to imply versions of each of my previously introduced element categories (*point, line, shape, space, color*).

———

A *point* is never alone in what it communicates. At the least it will convey a location and a color.

LINE

A *line* is the element message that delineates a single continuous primary dimension and direction. It is occasionally described as "the path of a moved point."

—

There are two fundamental types of *lines* (width and edge),

plus the previously suggested implied possibility that often relies on a series of *points*. Either may be communicated on a two-dimensional surface or as a part of three-dimensional circumstances. Either may have specific lengths with abrupt endings or no specific length if the ending gradually fades into the surface.

—

An **edge** *line* emphasizes one dimension and has no width. *Edge lines* populate all images and are easily ignored, but they should be corralled in a contributive way, just as any drawn *line* is consciously incorporated. *Edge lines* occur wherever two *colors* or shapes collide. If the two colors are very different from each other (black and white), the *edge line* will be particularly legible (hard). If the two colors are similar (light yellow next to white), the *edge line* will be quite subtle (soft). These exist in two- and three-dimensional situations. The edge of this page is an *edge line*. The edge of a table or a building is an *edge line*.

A **width** *line* emphasizes one primary dimension but also has the second (width) dimension. If those two dimensions replicate each other, a "shape" message is likely to overcome *"line."* The width factor additionally carries a color. This means that *width lines* are inherently less simple than are *edge lines*. A *width line* created by a three-dimensional circumstance need not have a color of its own (such as a floor plank or the side of a tabletop) but it still has an inherent color. *Width lines* may or may not have a specific width because of the opportunity to gradate (with color or dimension) one or both sides into the surrounding surface. When a *width line* is relatively wide, it will additionally reveal its bordering *edge lines*, thus compounding the communication (in fact, the *edge lines* that envelop a *width line* need not share its particular path, thus revealing some intriguing multiple direction options within a single *width line*).

—

There are two distinctively different *line* categories within both *edge* and *width* messages ("straight" and "curve").

—

Since my *line* definition incorporates a "single continuous primary dimension and direction," when directional changes occur in an otherwise straight message, it becomes more than one *line* (it is no longer singularly straight).

—

Curved *lines* are inherently more complex than straight *lines*, but the same "single continuous primary dimension and direction" notion is applicable. A curve is a linear message that possesses a continuously changing and successive direction. For this reason, there is no such thing as an S-curve—rather, this becomes a combination of two curves. Each is directionally successive until they connect. So an S-*line* message exists, but it is made up of two curves.

—

There are two kinds of line curves: circular and spiral.

A circular curve is when the degree of curvature is consistent. This curve has a mechanical character and can be easily produced, although circumstances may require optical correction in order to make it visually circular. It is repetitious in terms of its degree of curvature (this relates to my upcoming Harmony section).

—

A spiral curve is when there is an increasingly tighter (or looser) visual degree of curvature along its length. It is progressive in terms of its degree of curvature (this also relates to my upcoming Harmony section). Spiral curves are somewhat sensual because they emulate the curves in nature.

—

When a *line* alters its degree of curvature (consistent for circular and increasing for spiral), another *line* message is emerging. *Point* messages occur at such junctures and may be EXPLICIT (if there is an abrupt connection between two curves, two straights, or a curve and straight) or IMPLICIT (such as for an S combination when there is an otherwise quiet connection between two curves or, similarly, when a curve and a straight smoothly connect).

—

With single curves and multiple *line* combinations (straights and/or curves), there are two equally important directional

statements to manipulate in the service of aesthetics and communication: line direction and axis direction.

Line direction is the path of the *line* itself as previously described and is fundamentally self-evident. However, axis direction is an equally important factor. Axis direction is the core attitude of any *line* that incorporates two or more straights, one or more curves, or straight and curve combinations. This opens a new door in that an axis direction may be straight and/or curved no matter what linear vehicles cause it. For instance, it would be easy to communicate a straight axis direction with a connected or disjointed series of curves. Axis direction is often a more seductive or dominant message than are the *line* directions. In developing a finished design, it can be helpful to physically draw the axis directions (perhaps on an overlay tracing if using traditional materials), or at least imagine them, in order to manipulate them for correctness.

SHAPE

A *shape* message assumes recognition of an area's total contour/boundary. Enclosure exists, or is at least suggested by the ability to see most of its perimeter. If you move in close enough to any *shape* and can no longer see its boundaries, *space* and *color* become the perceived element messages. If you move far away from a *shape* or when it is very small, it is likely that *point* becomes the perceived primary element message. These notions reinforce my previously suggested relevance of the viewing situation.

——

It should again be acknowledged that the word "form" is sometimes defined as meaning what is being referred to here as *"shape."* Let's optimistically put that confusion to rest once and for all. Form and *shape* are different animals.

It is most appropriate to use the word "form" for the inclusive reference (as is introduced early in this text) that incorporates all of the element categories. Whether or not this is officially sanctioned from some linguists' point of view, it is a legitimately clarifying categorization in design/art. I believe that *"shape"* is an understandably descriptive word for this particular element component, just as "form" successfully denotes the extended visual family (*point, line, shape, space, color*).

The *shape* element category is important in two particular ways. First, shapeliness communicates with relative clarity. For instance, it may be easy for anyone to see the difference between two or more *shapes*, while not everyone could as easily distinguish differences between two different *colors* or *lines*. Consequently, *shape* distinctiveness is often paramount in the design of symbols and signs. The *shape* of a vehicle stop sign, rather than its *color* or language, is universally understood. Second, *shape* may be considered to be the most pluralistic of the element categories. Every shape is an overstuffed carcass in that it incorporates all of the other primary form elements: *color* (within its boundaries), *line* (whether edge or width), *point* (where straights and/or curves connect), and *space* (at least within its contour).

——

The simplest *shape* message, in terms of having such additional element baggage, is a circle. A pure circular *shape* minimally incorporates one circular *line*, a *color* within, neighboring and interior *space*, and an implicit *point* at its center. Every other *shape* has more going on.

——

There are two distinct kinds of designed *shapes.*

A **symbolic** *shape* is a *shape* with which we are familiar. It represents something else. This may be a pictorial representation (such as a star, a flower, a facial profile, etc.) or a previously learned image (such as geometric identities, pictograms, corporate symbols, etc.).

An **abstract** *shape* is a *shape* that creates its own unique identity as a pure form statement. Cloud-like or straight-sided rock-like forms imply such possibilities. It is very difficult to effectively design a fully abstract *shape* because humans are inclined to audaciously make seen things understandable by transforming abstractions into familiar themes. So in viewing that cloud-like abstract *shape*, many people will force it to represent something familiar (e.g., a kidney, rock, ghost, etc.).

Once an abstract *shape* becomes known to stand for something else, it has transformed into a symbolic *shape*. This occurs for corporate symbols, or even in our most common vernacular (e.g., a pentagon *shape* was abstract until it was so baptized).

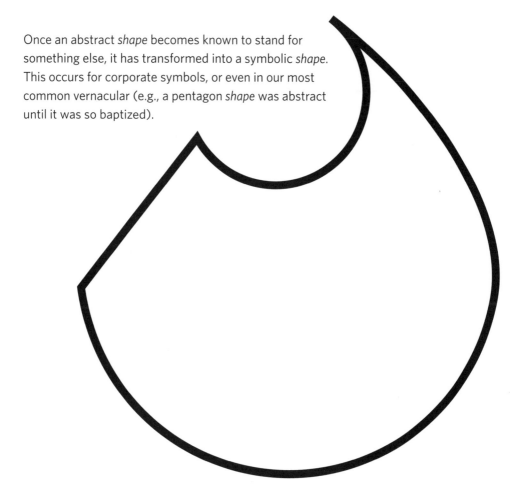

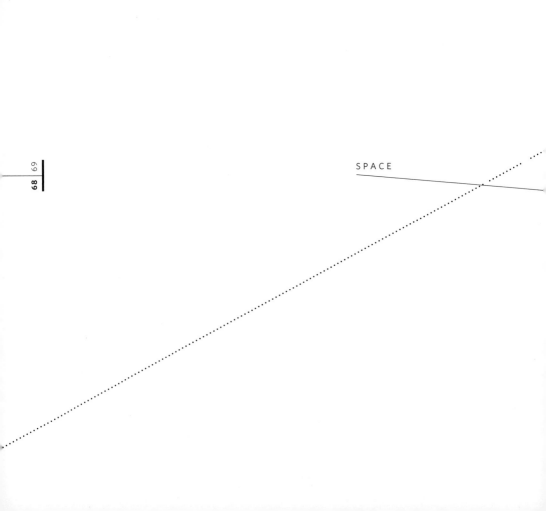

SPACE

Space is that stuff that is around, within, and between the other elements.

The previous *shape* category will, because of its innate complexity, become a player in this element category.

There are three distinct categories of *space*: two-dimensional, three-dimensional, and four-dimensional.

Two- and three-dimensional *space* are self-explanatory. It should, however, be noted that a given design may involve actual three dimensions or it may deal with implied three dimensions when communicated on a two-dimensional surface. Two-dimensional *space* is only actual. Of course, the *space* categories may coexist in a single item. Quantity is the primary control factor that we have with *space*.

The fourth spatial dimension is **time**. This is when a visual piece requires more than a singular view to be fully comprehended. It involves a seeing sequence that necessarily occupies time. When this sequence and the amount of time is prescribed by the designer, as with a movie title, it can be identified as having a "sequential viewing structure." When the sequence is determined by the viewer, as with a web page, it can be identified as having an "alternative viewing structure." In addition to such obvious kinetic media, all multiple component items are included. This covers such products as publications and exhibitions. Also, all actual three-dimensional designs necessarily incorporate four-dimensional *space* because for a full visual examination, the viewer cannot grasp their entirety from only one point of view. You must move around such items or have them rotate in your view, thus occupying time. Package designs fall into this arena in that a viewer only comprehends a complete impression as the result of seeing all sides and mindfully or subconsciously assembling a whole.

Some items can be designed for either a sequential or an alternative viewing structure. Reference books are purposely designed for alternative ease while novels are designed for sequential comfort. An exhibition may be designed to tell a story so that a viewer begins at one end and sequentially moves through to the exit—this can be dictated by the interior architecture or strongly nudged by how the visuals are orchestrated—or it may be done, with an alternative viewing structure, in a way that allows and encourages the viewer to comfortably wander back and forth from one component to another. With some sequential structures, the designer may predetermine the amount of time required for viewing (a film) or may allow the viewer this choice (a book). Given the explosion of visual systems as well as electronic and digital media, the fourth dimension of time has become an increasingly compelling designer obligation.

———

A popular term and concept within any art/design colony is "negative *space*." It generally refers to the openness that we see between images. This *space*, whether two-, three-, or four-dimensional, is important and is often ignored. It is like the critically delineated silences between musical notes or the poignant pauses in a performer's monologue.

In fact, negative *space* is often a heftier presence than are the obvious images that embrace it.

———

Most of us have encountered examples of the optical illusion where two symmetrical images create something like a vase, a face, or maybe a bawdier presence in the *space* between. Type designers honor such *spaces* within (counters) and between (fitting) letter-forms for the benefit of legibility as well as aesthetics. I will, with a minor dose of facetiousness, debunk a bit of this long-standing concept by suggesting that

there is no such a thing as negative *space*.

If something has a presence that is seen, it is a positive something. Perhaps we have been too reckless in adopting and furthering this well-meaning notion of there being such a phenomenon as nothingness. In any event, this is linguistic nitpicking so long as we acknowledge negative *space* as an aspect of visual form that is no less pervasive or potent than are *lines, colors*, etc.

—

I promised, at the beginning of this element category, to introduce some dual *space/shape* considerations. These tendencies for reading

three-dimensional *space* with a two-dimensional image
are somewhat applicable to other element categories
but become particularly evident with *shape*: If one shape
seems to overlap another, the overlapped is seen as behind
the other; if two similar *shapes* are different sizes, our
knowledge of perspective will suggest that the larger one
is closer to us; if the contour of one *shape* seems more
detailed than another, it may appear closer because we
are accustomed to more easily seeing the details of closer
items; a *shape* that is lower on a format will appear closer to
us because of our environmental conditioning; a primarily
convex shape will tend to appear more "positive" while a
primarily concave shape may appear as a "negative" hole in
the format; if the shape's contour is reminiscent of a known
volume (such as a cube), some such internal dimension will
be suggested.

—

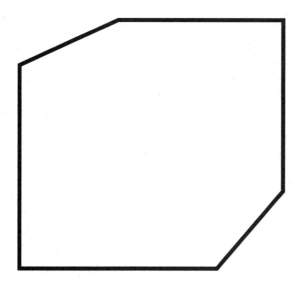

The following color element category also influences spatial communication: warm colors tend to come forward while cool colors tend to recede; bright colors tend to come forward while dull colors tend to recede; light colors tend to come forward while dark colors tend to recede.

All such considerations for shape or color do, however, depend on the particular circumstance at hand—it's always relevant.

COLOR

Color is the element that allows us to identify the differences and similarities between two or more otherwise undefined areas. It exists with all other elements and as a part of most. It is also the most intriguingly complex element category.

—

Color is perplexing because of its interpretive variability and its innate inconsistencies.

A given *color* is different when seen within or alongside other *colors*, in different lighting situations, in various quantities, and depending on each person's eyesight.

Additionally, there are a limitless number of *colors* and no one has the authority to pinpoint what the single purest version is of any given *color*. Also, different cultures, trends, individuals, ages, and professions project their own situational, learned, and emotional biases. *Color* is a peculiarly romantic element, given the universal attention that is lavished on it, along with its various personalized nuances and non-absoluteness.

———

Another point of consternation is that our commonly espoused *color* terminology is flawed as the result of its use and evolutionary lineage, much like a given story changes as it is passed through a series of people.

———

I will clarify and define some *color*-related terminology in order to, as the cliché goes, level our playing field. The term *"color"* is mistakenly but commonly used to describe the differences between green, blue, etc. This is wrong because such differences pinpoint just one of the three characteristics that cause a particular *color* identity.

The term *"color"* should be considered as an umbrella term,

while **hue** is the proper term to describe characteristic differences such as yellow, blue, green, orange, etc. The second characteristic is **value**. VALUE involves the visual (and perhaps the physical) addition or subtraction of white or black to a HUE. VALUE differences are often described as "lighter = tint" or "darker = shade." We can have a dark or a light VALUE of the same HUE. These two characteristics of HUE and VALUE are the most easily controllable and identifiable component characteristics of color.

———

A third color characteristic, somewhat contentious in that it is more difficult to manipulate and to decipher, is **chroma**. This word, and other terms that are often used to identify this characteristic, can also be confusing. They all suffer from varying definitions, assumptions, and connotations. Some of the related terms that are commonly used to identify this characteristic include brightness, intensity, saturation, luminosity, purity, and vividness. Given the innate challenge of understanding this component, "brightness" is relevant and self-descriptive, although this can also be misleading by favoring it over the equally legitimate but opposite term "dullness." In any event, a specific green HUE may have a light or a dark VALUE but also be dull or bright.

Each of these three characteristics involves a span of options. The traditional *color* wheel is the HUE span. Its circumference is huge with any number of specific points between red–purple–blue–green–yellow–orange and back to red. VALUES that run from white and through grays to black represent an elongated but more linear span. The CHROMA span is the shortest, and while it requires considerable practice in objective seeing to discern it and its difference from VALUE, it is also the most difficult to physically manipulate. A linear CHROMA span ranges from dull through mid-steps to bright.

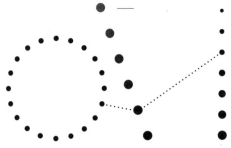

The CHROMA factor should not be confused with the concept of reflectivity or gloss. A shiny (glossy) surface is not necessarily brighter than a matte (dull) surface but it is likely reflecting (mirroring) lights, etc., in the environment rather than emitting more internal intensity.

———

Any given *color* is the result of bringing together one point on the HUE wheel with one point on the VALUE span and one point on the CHROMA span. This reveals that there are a limitless number of *colors* and a dizzyingly abundant number of options to create *color* harmony in a design, as will be explored in the next chapter.

———

I have previously alluded to the relativity aspect of *color*. This deserves further explanation. When two *colors* are placed together, they interact with and change each other (of course, this is a visual rather than a physical reality). This reciprocal interaction is most obvious when a small quantity of one *color* is placed within a larger quantity of another *color*. Essentially, what happens is that the characteristics that are shared by both *colors* are visually bled from the small-quantity *color* while, conversely, the characteristic components that are most different are consequently exaggerated. The large-quantity *color* bullies

the small-quantity *color*. Such characteristic components may involve HUES or VALUES—less so the CHROMA. This can best be witnessed when a small quantity of some *color* is placed side by side within larger quantities of two different other *colors*, but it occurs, at some level, for all adjacencies. This kind of interactivity is expanded as the result of a room's *color*—even the viewer's clothing—and especially the type of artificial or natural ambient lighting.

—

Another element message that is omnipresent with *color* is *edge line*. Our decisions concerning combinations of *colors* are accompanied by the intriguing baggage of such *line* messages and should, consequently, be considered as if we were drawing the more obvious *width lines*. When two very different *colors* collide, they create a very legible (hard) *edge line*. The legibility of such *lines* depends on the similarities and the differences of HUE, VALUE, or CHROMA between the two *colors*. The *edge line* hardness is a clue, in fact, as to the degree of difference between two adjacent *colors*. Two different *edge lines* may be equally legible as the result of a slight difference in any of the three *color* characteristics, or in some combination of them. Incidentally, this predicts useful harmonic opportunities that will be explored in the next chapter of this book.

AESTHETICS

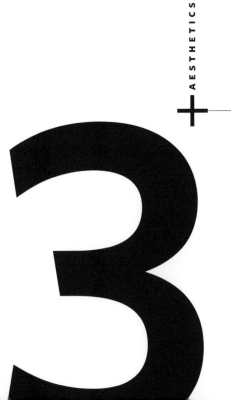

PREAMBLE

Aesthetics (or "esthetics") is "the artistry of an endeavor."

This term is applicable and may be differently defined in various fields, but here we are concerned with **design aesthetics**. *Design aesthetics* can be defined as

"the successful unification and satisfying expression of all of the components in a visualized whole." This introduces an antithetical objective of individuality for each ingredient along with a pluralistic togetherness.

―

"Design aesthetics" alludes to a **fundamental** concept of beauty rather than relying on our formulaic assumptions concerning what makes something attractive. A design's beauty does not dismiss but is not dependent on an obvious prettiness or a decorative frill.

Aesthetic beauty involves a combination of correctness

(appropriateness for the situation at hand),

uniqueness (something unexpected or original),

and harmony (all of the parts fusing together

to create a symphonic summation). This requires us to separate content-based recollections of beauty (flowers, doilies, bunnies, etc.) from the abstract visual form that is involved. We can admire, equally, the beauty of a rose as well as that of a racehorse or an automobile. Consequently, a photograph that depicts repugnant subject matter can still be an aesthetically beautiful image. Of course, this is not to say that appealing content cannot happily coincide with form beauty.

——

Three areas of consideration are embedded in each successful example of graphic design: syntactic, semiotic, and pragmatic.

Design aesthetics focuses on the **syntactic** component. It refers to the considerations that involve visual form and the interrelationships of its otherwise individualized elements. A predominate share of my writing favors the many aspects of such syntactic factors because they are the foundation constants of every design, no matter the assignment particulars or what tools or technology may be in use. Given its pervasive public neglect and the too-common artless indulgences, understanding the syntactic factors is a daunting challenge that requires some concerted attention by all of us.

——

The **semiotic** factor deals with the content (meaning or message) that is communicated in a given piece. The **pragmatic** factor deals with how well something functions (its legibility, permanence, cost, etc.). I will mostly rely on my esteemed colleagues' texts to elaborate on the semiotic and pragmatic categories. For that matter, there are also numerous other publications that expand on aspects of my foci.

Design aesthetics (syntactics) is essential to the quality of our lives. It ideally establishes an enriched legacy for advancement by our children's generation and beyond. We might easily be able to imagine how drab our mindset would be without any music, with foods that are nutritious but always bitter or that lack any taste, and with an absence of theatrical, dance, or comic performances. These things may not be objectively necessary for our day-to-day survival, but they are essential for a satisfying life. A dearth of tasty design aesthetics would produce a rancid existence. An important Bauhaus-inspired design quote is "form follows function." This asserts that the functional success of an item is paramount and should dictate how it looks. Its appearance should truthfully and simply reflect what it is and how it works. I agree, but I believe that when taken at face value, this oft-repeated rule of form following function is incomplete.

I suggest that

How something looks is critically important to our psyche and to civilization at large. Humans survive on the subsistence necessities of life but we are humanized by the *qualities* of what we taste, hear, touch, smell, and see. History mostly reveres the creative legacies of prior civilizations in the fields of art, design, literature, music, invention, science, etc. Beyond this, I propose that an overwhelming function for most of our objects, furniture, buildings, and images begs for environmental or sculptural enrichment. We spend much more time seeing each such item than we spend using them. We never set foot in most of the buildings that we encounter daily. The many urban signs that we walk past are, more often than not, primarily selling items and services to others. Objects, such as a coffeemaker or a toaster, occupy our peripheral vision for many more hours than they are employed. Consequently, in each situation, their form functions to beautify or uglify our lives and to inspire or to dampen our attitudes, thoughts, and actions while mirroring our personal and cultural standards.

Our neighbor who chooses wall art and mantel objects primarily to blend in with the furniture or wallpaper, or to emulate what's "in," demonstrates a shaky motive and knowledge. Similarly, those who rely on an interior decorator to furnish their homes would not likely hire a musician to dictate their entertainment or someone else to assign their readings, meals, sports, or movie preferences. Doing so is an admission of a personal design vacuum. Either situation reflects the relatively superficial perspective or inbred insecurity that so many people have concerning the visual arts versus most of life's other pleasures. However, such citizen innocence can be blamed on our education system and cultural conditioning, as opposed to us as individual decision-makers. I love America but suspect that people born and raised in Florence, Italy, are likely to have a somewhat more evolved "taste" for the visual world.

———

It is also reasonable to consider, consistent with the great architect Frank Lloyd Wright's point of view, that the things that we produce are no more unnatural than an oak tree. We create things and images that have been informed and inspired by our experiences with nature, and we channel our creations through our inherent God-given humanness. The designer's mind, heart, and soul are embedded in each resulting object. In concert with this, a dose of one's human quirkiness is endearing while helping to define the creator's individuality, adding warmth to what we do, and thus making man-made things more substantive and, ultimately, "natural" on their own terms. But too many visual choices and decisions are founded in what is customary or habitually safe. It's not uncommon for people to categorically dismiss "contemporary" design options in favor of nostalgia, even though today's most cutting-edge superior stuff is necessarily impregnated by ancestral benefactions, while furthering a legacy of creative license. It is meritorious to acknowledge and celebrate this moment while also cherishing the best of our past without mimicking it. Our earliest ancestors usually went beyond what was necessary to imbue each item (building, furniture, publication) with a level of beauty and craft that is seldom replicated in their parodied reiterations. Conversely, today's journeyman design work is too often primarily impelled by a deadline, digital ease, or a budget rather than any elevated ideals. The result is, too often, a cookie-cutter blandness.

HARMONY

A fundamental doctrine in every field of creative expression is the need for an effective balancing of "theme and variation" (or similarly, "unity and contrast") factors. **This is the essence of *harmony*.**

This section introduces some atypical but definitively commonsense postulations and is a critical component in this text.

———

Designers should strive for a balance where each visual ingredient is independently important while still contributing to the total composition. The objective is to fuse all of the ingredients into one whole. This is analogous to a successful family unit (which child would a parent first toss from the sinking ship?) where each person is equally important in his or her role while also contributing to a unique team dynamic.

———

Consider the elegant sport of rowing. Each athlete exerts tremendous individual power along with almost superhuman stamina while perfectly synchronizing every movement with one, three, or seven crewmates (sometimes plus a coxswain). The result, from the shore, appears to be beautifully effortless. The individuals become one with each other and with the shell, blades, and water.

———

Now consider a contentious mob circumstance where, in design, there could be visual anarchy. Sophisticated design attempts to achieve as much alliance as possible among all of the element ingredients, thus causing proper attention to be directed to the necessary differences. The unifying characteristics nudge us to appreciate the contrasts (variations) while the contrasting ingredients make the unity (theme) appreciable. This is an intriguing confrontation, while any noncontributory contrast (impostor) should be seen as collateral eye static.

—

There are two primary ways to create harmony of otherwise disparate elements: **repetition** and **progression**. Both are based on a fundamental notion of visual logic.

—

Repetition is the label for one harmonic way to unify elements. If two or more

different ingredients share (repeat) something such as the same color, size, location, etc., they are married (unified) in that way.

There must be at least two separate messages in order to use and appreciate harmony through repetition, but this is not a problem because, in effect, there are always at least two messages. The idea of repetition as a unifying tactic may be relatively easy to understand, and it affords many internally nuanced opportunities. When multiple lines are spaced equally, such a regular interval employs repetitious harmony. When two different items match in terms of their color's hue, value, or chroma, they are repetitiously harmonious (unified) in that way.

The more thematic unity through repetition there is, the more concise the contrasts and the consequent communication clarity will be. For instance, assume that our display objective is to promote a sculpture exhibition. It would make sense to emphasize three-dimensional form.

Imagine that we begin with a large shiny red ball in one room and a small dull black cube in a neighboring room. The more irrelevant differences that we discard, the better. Therefore, we place them side by side: both are colored a dull gray, and they are sized equally. They have been unified through such consistencies (repetitions of location, color, and size). This exaggerates the primary difference of shape (cube versus sphere). The result is a coexisting blend of unity with one appropriate contrast. This is harmony by means of repetition, and it dramatically directs attention to a clear communication of three-dimensionality in order to promote the sculpture exhibition.

—

The second way to unify multiple ingredients is **progression.** This method tends to be more difficult to tackle. However, it wonderfully allows the designer to achieve unity by how things differ. This seems like a contradiction but it is still rooted in the original visual logic precept. Here, we attempt to have the visual degree of difference between

three or more distinct items be appreciably methodical. This may occur within an element category or by commingling categories. The concept of **repetition** is actually part and parcel of this in that, in its primary application approach, there is a **repetition** of the DIFFERENCES between the element items as opposed to a *repetition* of the element items themselves.

A simple interval exercise with adjacent lines that gradually spread farther away from each other is an opportunity for a progressive interval harmony. Following are some other harmonic *progression* examples.

Imagine three line lengths: a two-inch, a three-inch, and a twelve-inch. There may or may not be repetition unity of their color, width, and certain other factors, but they are decidedly random in terms of length. If, however, the twelve-inch-long line is reduced to four inches, the degree of difference between it and the three-inch line echoes the degree of difference between the three- and two-inch lines (consistently a one-inch difference). In a way, the three-inch line becomes a bridge that brings unity to the group by sharing a consistent difference with the other two. They are magically unified in how they differ. Even if they are not organized from small to large, an underlying unity exists within that format.

———

The aforementioned theory can apply even if there are several lengths and if the momentum of a degree of difference's progression is consistent, such as with a Fibonacci sequence (one to two to three to five to eight inches, etc.). This momentum approach works only within an element category (line or shape or point or color). It is not applicable when commingling element categories (e.g., a degree of difference in line length that repeats the degree of difference between two colors).

———

It is necessary with progressive harmony to have at least three different item messages, so that the degree of difference becomes the unifying factor. If there are only two different elements, there is only one difference between the two and it cannot be conjoined with another.

—

These harmony tools can be played in fascinating ways. For instance, if the two-inch and three-inch lines are the same color and the twelve-inch line's color is altered just enough (in terms of the difference of its hue, value, or chroma) to an extent that visually duplicates the relatively minimal length difference between the two shorter lines, this interestingly meshes entirely different element categories through a progressive harmony (but remember, probably not if momentum is the determining factor).

—

This concept rationale may seem to be contrived, but it is no more of a stretch than the complex harmonic precepts that are similarly employed by talented concertmasters while weaving their compositions or the underlying formulas that inhabit the hard sciences. Audiences enjoy music without requiring the listeners to have conscious analytical knowledge. Indeed, I am likely to enjoy a fine restaurant entrée without being able to discern the ingredient portions or the chef's methods. It is reasonable to expect that the art/design fields can also employ such objective underpinnings that need not be consciously understood by the public in order to be sub- or unconsciously savored by everyone. Incidentally, it is possible for passionate designers to spontaneously employ such principles without mindful acknowledgment or formal education but rather as a result of their intensity and practice, much like the occasional self-taught genius in any field. A beginning student of design should, however,

consistently experiment with and consciously employ such principles to digest them and to succeed. Eventually, as with any oft-practiced exercise, they become second nature and are automatically employed and built upon. As a bonus, this initially thoughtful process nourishes one's critical thinking abilities beyond the task at hand.

The observer of a resolved design is likely to feel its harmonic correctness without mindfully understanding why it looks so appealing.

A perhaps secondary **harmony** concept that has seemed to robustly resonate with my students is my explanation concerning "spice." In order to have a perfect blend of everything in an image, each seen ingredient should be portioned correctly so that no one item overpowers unless such attention is intended. Simply put, those things that are

the most alike require larger portions while the most unique ingredients will hold their own in smaller quantities. If we liken this to a scrumptious salad, the lettuce and spinach need to be bulky in order to allow them each to be tasted, the tomatoes and cheese portioned less, the dressing even less, and any pepperishness very sparsely. The result will be a meshing where you may not even be able to decipher individual ingredients. The pepper-like ingredient is the spiciest and should be a tiny portion. Similarly, spice in a visual meal can be a yummy ingredient but must be controlled so as not to offensively overpower the design harmony.

Red socks may add some proper tang to enliven an outfit, while a red suit would be clownish. The context deserves some attention because, for instance, wildly plucky patterns on jockeys are compelling and apropos. Usually, however, when quantities are out of whack, ingredients battle with each other by shouting for independent attention. This idea of spice is most evident with color, but it applies to each element category and to form in general.

CREATIVITY

Creativity ideally means to germinate and produce ideas or things that are novel or unexpected but relevant to a goal, and that excite our physical, mental, emotional, or social existence. A creative design may be radical by opening previously unexplored territory for anyone to further navigate, or it may be subtle and personal for more exclusive ongoing inspiration. A seemingly minor creative insight will often act as a step forward and then be expanded in a subsequent opportunity.

Human beings are by nature creative, particularly when challenged, but talent manifests itself in various ways depending on each person's inclinations, education, skills, circumstances, opportunities, and experiences.

It is appropriate to review some primary nuances of the terms "creativity" and "art" because, contrary to some thinking, they are independent of each other but become most potent when combined (creative art/design). At its most fundamental level, art is anything that is done with an intent of personal expression, but an artistic piece may or may not be highly creative, much less elevate to the stature of high art that sparks new horizons for others.

High art stirs mysteriously visceral insights that awaken one's inner self.

It's a bit like our first-ever tasting of chocolate.

—

This is not to say that naive explorations are not self-gratifying and possibly skillful. Amateurs entertain themselves and others through the doing and the appreciating of personal expressions (visual, musical, etc.).

—

Applied design (functional work) can also become high art when it improves upon or solves a situation with cohesiveness and insight while opening new vistas and elevating our senses beyond the task at hand. Such revelations are most likely to be produced by people who have long focused and experimented in a particular design discipline, but random fireworks are always possible.

—

There is a secondary misconception that any visual that is created or is different exemplifies artistic creativity. Often, what we are fed is simplistic self-gratification. This is OK when done for one's personal appeasement as long as it doesn't masquerade as meaningful professionalism that is promulgated for others' stimulation or consumption. Anyone can produce something that is original, but this is a casual occurrence unless the product coincides with pertinence concerning an issue (self-inflicted or assigned) at hand, is aesthetically resolved, and touches our inner consciousness. We should not assume that any self-indulgence that a person creates (painting, drawing, sculpture, design) represents a creatively artistic achievement if our definition of art transcends its most baseline interpretation (a personal expression). For instance, at this most common level, any infant's crayon scribbles are correctly labeled as art. We know, however, that innocently expelled sounds, movements, or writings are usually not civilization-cherished examples of music, dance, or literature. For a piece to become creative art/design it must have contextual relevance in relation to a particular idea, question, or issue; it usually emanates from a substantial knowledge and skill set; it must have aesthetic poeticism; and the result should contain an intriguing depth that activates one's awareness, inspires further thought, and has lasting value.

We do seem to be stuck with this one term—art—that allows two legitimate but quite different interpretations. Message duality is not rare. In fact, it can be vexing that in all of our communication attempts (visual, audio, or editorial), recipients are likely to formulate an interpretation that deviates from the originator's point of view. This is because each viewer applies his or her own perspective and because the viewing environment and other circumstances influence meaning. This elevates the communication designer's challenge to strive for as much concise clarity

It is impossible to teach creativity in design, art, dance, or music but it is possible to foster the knowledge, confidence, and skills (motor as well as reasoning) that will help students develop and ultimately express their innate creativity. Studious discipline does not destroy latent creativity, much like initially learning to play "Chopsticks" followed by ever more elaborate pieces does the opposite of negating one's eventual musicianship.

as possible, unless the intent incorporates ambiguity. In fact, even when the objective might be to communicate confusion, this must be done in a deliberate way rather than by simply scattering imagery. Humans try to make sense out of whatever is seen, and since certain visual relationships are likely to innocently occur, any intended disarray requires conscious planning. A parallel in literature would be if an author wants to communicate the stupor of a character, he or she does not write while drunk but must have his or her wits at hand.

The most substantial solutions usually evolve out of a methodical series of logical actions and decisions that reflect someone's mature obsessiveness and a healthy portion of fearlessness. There exists some issue, question, or problem that poses a challenge as the starting point. Even when one seems to explode with a sudden idea, this is likely the manifestation of significant prior thought and experience. I will never, for instance, produce an innovation concerning the sciences, music, or mechanics because those are not my experiential ballparks.

———

Interestingly, the most wondrous result often seems to be particularly simple and predictable once it has been revealed. Overworked designs often signal a forced and noncreative episode. Likewise, a professional golfer's oft-practiced stroke may seem simple, natural, and effortless to the innocent observer.

———

It is somewhat frivolous to have, as one's primary objective, the creation of a masterpiece. That would likely be

counterproductive, as opposed to simply working to explore or to solve an issue while negotiating the inherent selections and creative episodes. Great art is usually the result of experienced and engaged practitioners who

We must respect the spontaneity and intuition that festers within everyone's libido. It's a good idea to absolutely cut loose every once in a while. This is difficult to do because of our innate cautiousness. However, when faced with either a new or a recurrent challenge, open-ended brainstorming of "anything goes" can facilitate cathartic creativity. Even creative designers often fall into the trap of automatic assumptions and decisions (doing what is predictable).

are involved much like the most determined blue-collar laborers. Procedural concentration, along with know-how, presents the opportunity for a creative design to blossom. Masterful works emerge as the result of dedicated thought and actions that are inspired by externally or personally imposed challenges. These are fostered by a knowledge base in combination with a genuine old-fashioned work ethic. Just do the job at hand as well as possible, and if some magic occurs—bingo. When painting, sculpting, designing, etc., most of us cannot squeeze out great works of art for their own sake whenever we wish. Occasionally, a piece transcends what has been previously experienced and awareness is heightened.

—

It is interesting that we sometimes apply blanket credit to successful artists/designers and assume that anything that they do is majestic. Professionals spend a great deal of their time investigating and practicing with the realization that occasional masterpieces may occur. This does not deny the likely elegance of virtually anything that is produced by dedicated practitioners. The experience and personal confidence that is fostered by success does feed one's subsequent work, and it nourishes the likelihood of continuous mastery. When someone has done significant work, his or her confidence grows and this facilitates the possibility of perpetual success. This is like an athlete being "in the zone." However, there is no shortcut without paying the dues, just as is the case in any compelling endeavor. Confidence breeds success, but every performance by a superior musician or every novel by an acclaimed author is not automatically great.

—

Everyone who is seriously involved is likely to interrupt their creative chapters with some occasional hiccups. If there are no missteps, it probably means that one is not pushing beyond previous efforts and may simply be playing it safe by repeating the acceptably sure thing.

There are always alternatives.

METHODOLOGY

***Methodology* refers to a designer's creative or problem-solving process.** The most important and often difficult dual challenge is to determine a starting point and the very next step. Some renegades may best advance through a messy (random) but ultimately successful course of action, but most of us should begin at the most obvious and accessible bottom rung. If the designer can effectively identify what the most logical and simplest first two steps should be, the remaining process is likely to unfold naturally while the designer, like a travel guide, maneuvers and nudges everything toward a proper crescendo. At the same time, an innate process ownership and elasticity allows us to periodically revisit the earlier rungs.

———

It is a common rookie mistake, when faced with a new challenge, to try to immediately jump to a solution. That would be like a music composer fully birthing an opera based on someone's preliminary proposition.

There needs to be a give-and-take, like **a dialogue, between the designer and the objective, his or her thoughts, the tools, and the visuals.** In fact, it would be premature to leap forward purely on the basis of one's previous experience, plus the perfunctory briefing, rather than combining one's knowledge along with a full engagement in the particulars of the problem at hand, thereby nurturing a truthfully tailored solution.

———

Creative problem solving usually requires investigation, testing, experimentation, and critical reasoning, along with some jazzy improvisation, as opposed to solely expecting an insular middle-of-the-night awakening (although one's recall of unanticipated sleep-induced gems can, occasionally, goose the next day's advancement).

—

If a designer begins at the most obvious point and methodically progresses one step at a time, a final, unpredictable design will likely emerge. This design solution is not the result of one brilliant thought (although such profound creative impulses may inspire the project) but is the culmination of a series of rational choices, insights, and decisions along the way. This is not to say that the designer's individuality or creativity has been replaced

An evolved designer is not likely to produce what his or her clientele expects. As with any respected surgeon, a symptom should first be identified and then followed by the professional's diagnosis. However, many clients are likely to innocently ask for a poster, a brochure, or whatever—probably even suggest the imagery or concept—rather than more properly pose the issue. Design pros must judiciously negotiate this encounter.

ABOUT**DESIGN**

by pure objectivity. Any person similarly engaged with the identical issue would make different decisions while combining these with his or her personal insights and inclinations and arrive at an entirely different finale.

One of the provocative things about artistry is that there are an infinite number of appropriate and, indeed, ingenious solutions for every challenge. *Objectivity* and *creativity* should be recognized as complementary terms that cannibalize each other in a healthy way.

It may be human nature to begin a project with hyped enthusiasm and inventiveness, but such energy gradually diminishes as the end approaches. Instead, we should attempt a continuous series of energetic bursts, almost as though one is constantly beginning anew. This is like the workings of an internal combustion engine.

The particular problems/ issues/difficulties must be embraced as though they are opportunities, because they are.

Once a designer is able to clearly define the primary obstacles, resolution paths will be unveiled. Each difficulty can be seen as a fascinating door that requires a proper key. A designer will often discover an unexpected solution by concentrating on, exploiting, and even commingling the difficulties that are unique to a given situation. Rather than hiding or avoiding the barriers, we adopt them and transform them into a solution. Any edginess should stimulate the search.

Eventually, the designer is likely to reach a place where every reasonable avenue has seemingly been traversed and a satisfactory solution has emerged, but this may parallel satisfaction without an actual climax. Up to that satisfactory point, despite some speed bumps, we may assume that most of the steps have been relatively obvious to the designer. Nevertheless, this should be valued because problem-solving individuality has occurred.

Playfulness should be integral to the design process for the delight of the designer as well as adding some approachability for his or her eventual audience. Humor is almost always welcome and welcoming.

⌐ABOUT**DESIGN**

However, if there is time, inclination, and ability to continue the investigation and try to **push beyond this wall of basic gratification, there is the possibility for creative ecstasy and a rare eloquence.** This is elusive, but if one digs into the essence of the situation, one may create something special and inspire a new level of intrigue for the designer, if not the audience or peers. This supposedly unnecessary extension of the process is most likely when some epic insight may occur, but it is a rare encounter, even for advanced designers. One of the groovy things about this is that after a person has experienced such a transcendence, he or she is less likely to be too quickly satisfied in the future. Here lies the promise for elevated satisfaction and inspiration that creates an inner joy that is not unlike one's first romance. Sometimes premature breakthroughs unexpectedly erupt early on, and it takes an alert wisdom for someone to acknowledge and capitalize on such happy accidents.

It is not uncommon to blindly make automatic assumptions on the basis of previous encounters. For instance, I occasionally assigned students to select a particular restaurant and design a new menu. Inevitably, the food categories and item organizations would initially emulate existing menus, while the cover would picture the venue along with the address and telephone number (even though diners know where they are). I then challenged the students: If there is commonly an older clientele, should the items instead be categorized according to price, ingredients, digestibility, calories; if it is a hotel's restaurant, should visualizations be paramount to benefit non-English-speaking travelers; how about sight-impaired customers or dietary limitations? Avoid autopiloting a design.

There are happy accidents, but such accidents evolve with experience. I know that I am now better able to recognize and use the difference between "happy" and "unfortunate" accidents than I was as a beginner and that I am now more likely to father what others might assume was purely accidental.

COMPOSITION

To compose means to assemble different things within a design, whether one format or a related bunch. An effective composition requires that the many often diverse components be **harmoniously** combined. There are various organizational concepts that can help to accomplish this task. The two factors usually determined by the designer are the modules and their grouping. Modules refers to individual elements (i.e., points, lines, shapes) or more compound components such as photographs, symbols, typographic units, drawings, or other images.

—

Certain organizational considerations will facilitate **grouping** the **modules** into a harmonious whole (composition). The primary tool for achieving this is commonly referred to as a grid (or grid system).

———

The most traditional typographic approach is to have each sentence centered below the previous line of copy, thereby introducing a single centralized grid axis (an imaginary line) that serves to hold the individual sentences together. This is much like the horizontal axis that attaches each of these words to produce a linear connection for the ease of reading.

———

Along with every composition, there is a communication nuance at play that causes one or a combination of three visual statements. These three have to do with the visibility (legibility, obviousness) of either the individual modules or of their grouping.

———

1

When the way that things are grouped (composed) is more legible than are the individual modules, a *textural* statement occurs. I am primarily referring to a visual as opposed to a physical texture. In this case, we do not discern any distinguishing module uniqueness because their individuality is defeated by our seeing the overall group.

2

When there is equal legibility (importance) of the modules and the grouping, a *patternistic* statement occurs. Imagine any common pattern, such as may be seen in clothing or drapery, and note that there is likely this equivocal competition between the whole and the individual components. This notion is similarly evident in "figure/ground" studies where the positive ingredient competes for attention with the negative space. The particular viewing situation plays a role—so, for instance, a patternistic statement can best be achieved in a controlled situation such as for a handheld publication. Incidentally, a design that is seen from a distance may state texture since the individual components are not discernible, but as one approaches the design, we reach a point where pattern may dominate because there is equality. If we move even closer, it is possible that the following third statement occurs.

3

When the design's modules are more legible than the underlying composition (grouping), we have the most common statement. It also tends to be a more complex but intriguing circumstance. This is a *skeletal* statement in that it operates much like our human

skeleton, which serves as an underlying structure that holds everything in place, but its presence should usually not dominate. The most successful

skeletal statement is achieved when we retain a level of

composition legibility that complements and is in support of the modules' legibility. This replicates our common attitudes concerning human health and beauty. If the grid is overcome by the modules, an uncomfortably obese design emerges. Equally, if the grid is dominant, an uncomfortably emaciated design results.

———

Some naysayers feel that the use of a grid is unnecessarily limiting and that it reduces creativity by imposing structural rules. However, consider that humans share very similar skeletons but no two people are alike. In fact, our individuality is appreciated because of our commonality (theme and variation/unity and contrast). Similarly, buildings often share similar framing while expressing external or internal diversity. There are numerous instances where a grid may be imposed in graphic design for consistency's sake (magazine or branding systems), but it can be very helpful for the designer to initially employ an appropriate grid for any new assignment. When thoughtfully conceived, the grid is a creative component and is likely to emerge as a natural by-product during any mindful design process. A grid will facilitate pertinent experimentation and resolution in place of an otherwise infinite storm of options.

———

Grid unity (compositional harmony) is achieved through *positional* and *unit* relationships and repetition.

—

Positional relationships: It is not necessary, while employing a grid, to attach one item to another in order for them to be united. If they are, instead, aligned on a common (probably imaginary) grid line, they will visually connect. This is similar to human social interactions, where it is not necessary to grab on to someone. When one person in a crowded room points toward or even looks at someone else, everyone understands the connection. Similarly, in design we can effectively have modules "look" at each other to achieve organizational unity.

—

Unit relationships: This refers to size or length factors. When an established length is repeated, the two or more occurrences are unified. As an example, imagine a nine-square grid (9" x 9") that is made up of 3" square units. Each unit relates to every other unit. Beyond this, the more obvious incremental components (3"x 6", 3" x 9", etc.)

unify as a result of the original grid construction. If smaller components are necessary, logical incrementalization will help to maintain some level of unity. In the described example, particularly since the original grid was nine squares, one-third divisions of each 3" units provide the most logical additional options (1" or 2").

—

A well-conceived grid will provide a diverse but appropriately controllable menu of options for the placement of modules as well as their sizing. Using any of the

options assures some level of unity. Without the grid device, the investigation is arbitrary and unity will be more elusive because there is a mind-numbing array of choices available. The grid should be exploited to whatever extent possible but, when necessary, the designer has created this Frankenstein's monster and has license to override it. However, when an inordinate number of contradictions occur, we may assume that the grid was not initially well conceived or that the designer is being too casual in its use.

—

Limitations should be embraced as opportunities.
Reasonable limitations are the particular things that cause us to focus on a challenge, which then help to fabricate the particular result, and that are likely to make it engaging and legitimately successful in relation to the task.

—

There are three types of skeletal grids: compositional, tailored, and
dynamic. In most cases, a single design will likely employ a combination of two or three types.

—

A **compositional grid** is one that is created in advance of knowing what the modules will be, so the modules are eventually arranged, sized, etc. in ways that will, to whatever extent possible, fit into the grid units. The grid primarily offers a way to compose and to size the modules.

—

A **tailored grid** is created in response to some or all of the modules that already exist. The grid is constructed by the things that it will accommodate, like creating a newly fitted suit. This is often based on the primary rectangular proportions that occur with the modules. So, if different modules share a given proportion, that probably becomes a primary grid unit and it may dictate the design's overall proportion. Such proportions might be based on the module perimeter or a dominant component thereof (for instance with a photograph of a house, the overall photo creates one rectangular option but the outline of the house might offer another). Any remaining modules that do not share in the dominant proportion will treat the field as a compositional grid. This is not to suggest that a carefully constructed grid need be absolutely rectangular or straight sided, and certainly grids often expand beyond two dimensions.

—

A **dynamic grid** is where some forceful lines or alignments within modules are used to "point" to and, thus, unify with other modules (for instance, a photo of a soaring airplane would encourage that strong diagonal exhaust line to visually connect with other ingredients in the format). The organizational structure spontaneously occurs as a result of internal image commands. Similarly, sizes, lengths, and proportions that are internal to a module may become the dynamic "language" of a design.

It is common and particularly useful to develop an appropriate grid when designing the format for publications, web pages, etc. The grid system needs to graciously accommodate proper amounts of space and the relationships between the columns of typography (while considering readability factors), headlines, peripheral items such as subtitles, other imagery (such as photographs), and the spaces around such material. When designing a book, the gutter (spacing between the content and the book's binding) and even the sensitive incorporation of page numbers are important considerations that will elevate legibility, structure, and appeal.

In keeping with this subject, proportion pops up as a topic for consideration. This is because while grids may be constructed with irregular units, quite often the units are fundamentally rectangular where proportional factors are dominant. However, proportion considerations are also present with non-rectangular situations.

I suggest that a square is the most popular and functional rectangular proportion. It has many advantages. It is innately unified because its two dimensions *repeat* each other. Its dimensions are neutral so that it can be placed, with equal ease, into a horizontal or a vertical format and, as a format, it does not impose a dominant dimension. It is the one proportion that is immediately understood, which means that the viewer feels some level of initial subconscious affinity. It can flexibly be built with or subdivided. It is compatible with related proportions such as a double square or a two-to-three proportion. In fact, most other favored rectangles are cousins of the square. These include root rectangles and, most notably, the classic "golden" proportion. All such proportions are easier to work with because of their innate harmony and because the difference between their two lengths is not wishy-washy. Design decisiveness is always advantageous. Even when one intends subtlety, it should be done decisively so as to avoid an unintended ambiguity.

EDUCATION

4

OVERVIEW

First, a few of the clichés. "Education is ongoing." "We learn from our mistakes." "We teach ourselves more than we learn from others." All absolutely true, but an untruth is the too-common assumption that formal education is not necessary, or perhaps not even possible in art/ design, because people either have "it" or they don't.

Baloney. The preceding chapters outline some of the many teachable objective principles that facilitate one's problem-solving and creative capabilities while helping to avoid some of the toxic stuff. Much like a musician or an athlete, once we can control the equipment, are knowledgeable concerning history plus our various options, and can exercise optimum and varied skills, we are then free to express, experiment, and innovate.

Freedom comes from experience, knowledge, and practice, practice, practice.

Following is the transcription of a popular keynote address that I gave for a symposium at the University of the Arts (UA, previously identified as PCA—the Philadelphia College of Art). This event celebrated the fortieth year of its graphic design major. This monologue was extensive and a bit scrappy, so I hope that readers will forgive a few content overlaps with my other material, as well as any editorial sloppiness that is inherent to my having initially verbalized it. I feared that any deliberate or fussy doctoring now could accelerate on itself and that I might, consequently, exorcise its original spirit . . .

I **hate** being here for a forty-years celebration . . .

For me, it means that several in my fraternity, whom I love and admire for having played key roles in shaping graphic design education in America, are edging past or close to retirement. This place is a superior example and I am proud that some of my most talented former students have contributed here as faculty. Over the last forty years I have always praised PCA/UA as having one of the two or three finest programs around. That has been because of the unique confluence of visionary leadership, a consistently exceptional faculty, a wise program, gifted students, a supportive institution, and appropriate geography. It's an unfortunate rarity that such an educational chemistry is planted and continues to excel over four decades. Many schools, during this time, have sprouted but not blossomed, and I believe that the perennialness of a curriculum is essential for true excellence. Also, the faculty here have been sterling contradictions to George Bernard Shaw's claim that "he who can, does; he who cannot, teaches."

I'm not a historian, but since I now have lived almost fifty of my years in graphic design programs, I will share a broad-brush and somewhat freeform personal perspective, despite having a clichéd apprehension of preaching to the choir. I'll glance back a bit even though, in 1974, Billie Jean King said, "what usually makes people choke on any stroke is thinking about the past instead of the future." I'll also sneak in some related observations and opinions, since I'm licensed to do so given that they titled my talk "Connections."

In the beginning was the word **(form follows function)**. That was a pretty good seed for our modernist pioneers and for the first wave of related schools in the US. Most notably the New Bauhaus and Institute of Design, Black Mountain College, and Yale beginning in 1950. These involved classy people like Alvin Lustig, Josef Albers, Alvin Eisenman, Maholy-Nagy, and his pal, György Kepes. Realizing what those guys did might cause many of us to suffer an inferiority attack. Indeed, PCA had its own precocious but unconsummated early flirtations with real graphic design, by way of Alexey Brodovitch and, a little later, Armin Hofmann.

I don't mean to ignore the fact that many other even earlier and ongoing programs existed and that some had fine ingredients. They used titles such as advertising design, commercial art, or "art in industry" in 1927 at my own university. Such titles reflected what was **generally** a vocational mindset, as opposed to a broad professional problem-solving education versus training mentality. Several years ago I wrote, in an AIGA annual, "In 1955 I was a pudgy teen who hid out at the movies, where I remember being startled by Saul Bass' sassy titles for *The Man with the Golden Arm*. I eventually learned that I had encountered a unique example of **graphic design**. I cannot say that this experience persuaded me to pursue the field, but the fact that its mood registered on my naive psyche and that I retained this particular memory attest to the lasting impact of excellent design."

The common curricular tactics in this country, prior to the late sixties, tended to emphasize assignments that worshipped industry and were cloaked like dreaded artificial wood-grain, as though they were workplace jobs, while implying that education is not something that is **real** in and of itself, despite the fact that Josef Albers once wrote, "School isn't a place to make art but where we prepare for art work that may come after school." Result-oriented portfolio classes were paramount; students experienced brief crowd-critiqued charades with faculty who voiced subjective generalizations and opinions; skills were often divorced from thought; photos were rectangles above or below the type; mention of a grid and, for that matter, any objective reasoning was seen as an evil assault on creativity; and sparse academic courses were watered down so as to be comprehensible to the flaky art students. Institutional structures fostered a second-class attitude toward the capitalistic designers. The fine artists, in independent art schools, and the art historians or sometimes architects, in universities, ruled budgetary and program matters because design programs were cowering within such academic units. Even as a student at Yale in 1963, my sense was that it was more about inspiration by brushing shoulders with some heroes than it was about systematic teaching and learning. In defense, however, Yale was a lonely MFA concept at the time. This was why they invented what was termed "babygraphics" as an introductory-year encounter. I'm afraid that many university structures are still not particularly friendly with what we might consider the ideal concerning design.

In any event, thank God for the **eventual** emergence of a philosophically grounded educational progression, process over product, critical and articulate analysis, and academic substance within some undergraduate neighborhoods.

This did not mean the ignoring of one's personal dialect and intuitionism, but rather it provided the knowledge and the potential confidence that is necessary to effectively solve problems and to evolve independently. This signaled a transformation from design training to education, but we still had a long way to go. It reminds me of an interview I once heard with Billy Joel, who said, "I feel as though I am competent as a songwriter, musician, and singer and I have a theory that when you're competent but you live in an age when there is a lot of incompetence it makes you seem extraordinary." TV's *American Idol* auditions may reinforce such an attitude.

My dictionary defines "education" as the act or process of imparting knowledge or skill through systematic teaching It defines "training" as making proficient with specialized instruction and practice. A key word in the education definition is "knowledge," which refers to cognitive or intellective mental components acquired and retained through study and experience. This means that the mind is necessarily central. Another important aspect of the education definition is the systematic notion. The training definition implies something narrower in scope and does not necessarily require an orderly synthesis, but usually a repetitious practice, like a tiger jumping through a burning hoop. The mind is not challenged. Repetition, or training if you will, is certainly an ingredient in the educational process, but education is not inherently an ingredient when training.

I suggest that the small but infectious wave of true **undergraduate** graphic design pedagogies, most notably beginning with Rob Roy Kelly's graphic design department at the Minneapolis College of Art & Design in 1957, inaugurated an education coup. Rob was an energetic, brilliant, and principled man who had studied in one of Yale's first graduate graphic design classes and became a primary originator of key initiatives that so many of us now take for granted. These include the essence of sequentially oriented undergraduate graphic design studies, incorporating a critical mass of faculty and students. Rob championed community outreach projects, affirmative action, faculty working together as a design studio, and graphic design history. He was a catalyst for such notions along with team teaching, the integration of photography, and nonvocational course titles. I happened to be one of his first students. In 1964 Rob moved to the Kansas City Art Institute, where he became ever more pivotal for the state of undergraduate design education. There, he embellished the aspirations that he had introduced in Minneapolis and proactively recruited a faculty blend of Yalies with other ideologies including, most importantly, the first instances of faculty to come from Basel to the benefit of BFA students. The first hires worked out pretty well: Inge Druckrey in 1966 and, a year later, Hans-Ulrich Allemann. I was lucky to be a part of the team from 1965 to '68.

Independent art schools attended to the establishment of graphic design as a curricular component before most universities but, as universities gradually addressed more of the nonarchitecture design fields, their inclusiveness and ivory reputations helped to inspire a growing respect for the nuances of our field.

The times just prior to 1965 were contentious, but the world was headed toward an even sexier period. Most all designers, no matter what their style, had been educated in the fine arts because there were so few academic units that were dedicated to design, and the kids that did study it likely encountered my previously mentioned parochialness.

Modernist design firms like Unimark in Chicago and Brownjohn Chermayeff & Geismar in New York sprouted;

Armin Hofmann—who had godfathered Basel as of the late '40s—began a yearly teaching pattern at Yale and established a postsecondary-level graphic design program at Basel in 1968. In the field, there was growing awareness of multicultural communications and design systems in general—for instance, environmental design activities and many high-profile corporate programs emerged.

Realistically, graphic design education in America was still in an adolescent stage between a trade identity and a full-fledged profession, despite the fact that symbolic and typographic sophistications had shared a long heritage. One day back in 1787, Benjamin Franklin became the first American fan of Bodoni's typeface while working in his printing shop here in Philadelphia. *Print Magazine* was going strong since 1940, which is the decade that Phil Meggs described as the "incubator for modern American graphic design," but *Print* didn't have much company. I wonder what the unparalleled *Portfolio* magazine—art directed by Frank Zachary, designed by Alexey Brodovitch, and published in Cincinnati—*of course*—would be like now if it had survived beyond its three issues in the fifties. It folded because they decided to exclude advertisements out of fear that the designs would compromise their mission. We had to wait until the mid-eighties for Phil Meggs's book (*A History of Graphic Design*), which was our first truly scholarly history, and there weren't many other serious books or journals for our field; one yearly national conference was inaugurated in 1951 (the International Design Conference in Aspen) and few postgraduate study opportunities existed; the American Institute of Graphic Arts was essentially a New York City club with a couple chapters, although it had been around since 1914; few citizens knew what graphic design was.

So, around this time, an irreversible Swiss movement toward the good old U. S. of A. heated up. Their grounded confidence fertilized education with a disciplined, thoughtful approach to form. Amin Hofmann's poetic approach to process and the elements of visual form at Basel was consistent with Josef Albers's methodical, objective, and communications-oriented approach to color and other basic design studies. Inge, Hans, Ken Hiebert, Steff Geissbühler, and their colleagues did not, however, simplistically parrot what they had learned. They expanded from it and articulated in newly relevant ways for American students. The Swiss helped to replace our Velveeta-cheesy educational practices.

As we are well aware, in 1967 Ken Hiebert initiated a Basel-informed philosophy here, and consequently many of us feel that PCA became the **third** official and genuine undergraduate department of graphic design in the US, following Minneapolis and Kansas City. One year after that, I did likewise in forming such a department at the University of Cincinnati and also incorporated some of the Basel qualities.

That was the volatile year of 1968, when the Viet Tet Offensive caused Americans' war approval to suddenly plunge to 26 percent, Lyndon Johnson dropped out of the presidential race, Martin Luther King Jr. was assassinated, race riots burned in 130 cities, students seized universities, Robert F. Kennedy was assassinated, prisoners rioted as did demonstrators at the Democratic Convention in Chicago, and Richard Nixon was elected. Also, our astronauts became the first men to fly around the moon, the topless bikini was invented, the play *Hair* incorporated full-frontal nudity, gay life was portrayed in the play *The Boys in the Band* while Dustin Hoffman was seduced by a bored housewife. Kids, in the throes of sex, psychedelic drugs, and rock-n-roll were preaching not to trust anyone over thirty, and O. J. Simpson won the Heisman Trophy.

Lo and behold, in the midst of that Rob Roy Kelly, Ken Hiebert, myself, and a few others shared aspirations of elevating our playing field by layering into a logical and sequential educational building process with an emphasis on visualized investigation, as opposed to an artificial product or client worship; uncompromising excellence in every way possible—most certainly including personnel; full utilization of class time with diligent faculty/student interactions; a continuous dialogue of doing-thinking-seeing; an appreciation for subtleties and continuous creativity; encouragement of our students to encounter and be influenced by great art, music, architecture, etc. in order to avoid the likelihood of imitation when one dwells, with blinders, only on other examples of graphic design; and recognition of the importance of effective teaching from the beginning levels onward as opposed to glamorizing the senior courses. Seemingly simple assignments revealed and caused complexities of thought and understanding. I fear that even now, few imitators realize how

critical-visual experimentation and articulation can foster rational thought as opposed to simply

making things pretty. It can feed

the solution and cause complex knowledge that impacts
conceptualization and semiotics. Rather than biblically
repeating that form follows function, our Swiss friends
helped to suggest, as Paul Rand always preached, that

form and content are inseparable

(you can't have one without the other). Our challenge is
to effectively fuse them.

I acknowledge that, parallel to or quickly subsequent to
Minneapolis, Kansas City, Philadelphia, and Cincinnati,
there were healthy initiatives elsewhere—for instance,
RISD where, in 1970, Tom Ockerse added vigor with his
own presence plus doses of some compatible Dutch
stimulation, Malcolm Greer had preceded him there ten
years earlier, IIT, several New York and West Coast schools,
Roger Remington at RIT, Lanny Sommese at Penn State,
Indiana—first with George Sadek and eventually with Tom
Coleman—Bob Swinehart at Carnegie-Mellon in 1971, Kent
State had already adopted J. Charles Walker, Dick Dahn had
moved into the University of Washington in 1965 and was
later joined by Doug Wadden, both Peter Megert at Ohio
State and Phil Meggs at Virginia Commonwealth emerged

in 1970. All of those contributors were fleshed out with other eloquent faculty who I probably should but will not try to list. People like Jay Doblin, Lou Danziger, Meredith Davis, and Dietmar Winkler. Certainly, I cannot ignore the verve that was added by the McCoys at Cranbrook beginning in 1971. At Cincinnati, I have enjoyed the crucial quad-decades camaraderie of colleagues Joe Bottoni, Heinz Schenker, and Stan Brod, joined along the way by valued others including, now, Robert Probst, Maureen France, Kristin Cullen, and Sandy McGlasson.

Our whole field, in terms of having developed, dialogued, debated, and documented, concerning a body of knowledge, is relatively young. The first known use of the term "graphic designer" was in a 1922 article by W. A. Dwiggins in the *Boston Evening Transcript*, and dictionary definitions surfaced much more recently. I suppose that this is why there remains some nervousness about the very title "graphic design." Some want to leave it behind like gum on the bottom of a desk. Frankly, I find most of the proposals of alternative terms to be as distracting but irrelevant as is *Sports Illustrated*'s swimsuit edition. I think that we should gratefully accept what our forebears did while contending with the new issues, and avoid the pothole of rehashing our nomenclature. The term "graphic design" has become more inclusive than simply meaning the design of graphics. Why toy with terms like "visual communication design" (as was proposed in an Icograda design education manifesto in 2000) or even "visual engineer," which had briefly surfaced in the fifties? A term like "information architecture" sounds a bit pompous to me while leeching onto a peer profession's identity, but I suppose that it's OK as a **specialty** within the breadth and dignity of the profession of **graphic design**. Also, I strongly feel that trying to adopt a descriptive title, such as "communication design," is a juvenile sign of insecurity and that such terms carry their own euphemistic baggage. Our broad professional agenda allows for one or a blend of three primary purposes for any piece of graphic design: to inform or to persuade or to express, whether two-, three-, or four-dimensional. Would it help other professions to adopt more descriptive titles such as musicians becoming sound makers or would we feel more confident if the person in front was called an airplane driver rather than a pilot? The current definition in *Merriam-Webster's Collegiate Dictionary* may not be ideal, but it is decent, respectful, and not limiting. It is: "The art or profession of using design elements, such as typography and images, to convey information or create an effect"—although, interestingly, they claim that the earliest recorded use in English was in 1935. My own definition is that "graphic designers diagnose communication needs in order to conceive and to create an effective and socially responsible visual dialogue." Incidentally, this line of thought may help add credibility to my opinion that there is no single ideal curricular agenda for all schools. Our field is pluralistic enough to allow for, even require, varied philosophical bents and content emphases. Each place needs to objectively exploit its own unique potential.

We do eventually tire of trendy terminology such as inter- or multi- or cross-disciplinary. How about paradigm, branding, 110 percent effort, breaking news, and ultimate Doppler—or, closer to home, narrative or interface, perhaps even sustainability and digital design? On that note: I cannot count how many times I have been questioned, beginning in the mid-seventies and continuing now, about our integration of the computer—**get serious**: that issue became passé twenty-five years ago. In **1981** Apple computer's earnings increased 237 percent. **Of course** it is the most exponentially significant, promiscuous, and knockoff-friendly thing that we have encountered. In the hands of a knowledgeable and creative protagonist, it is a grand tool and interactive media that greatly enhances experimentation, efficiencies, and opportunities. But one of the attributes of our field is its evolutionary health and the fact that graphic design has consistently embraced new opportunities (from cave-marking tools to printing equipment to photography to digital technology). I spent many hours entrapped by an exotic dinosaur known as a copy camera. In education, one of the issues had always been how to fit in the new stuff and what is edited out in the process. My advanced students are digital **savants**, but I want to plead for a reasonable retention of basic design studies along with some fundamental hand skills. This has been one of the legacies of the real estate that we're honoring today. I still believe that with pencil and scissors and brush, there is an essential binding of mind-eye-hand and, thereby, a more likely digestion of understanding than if students are expected to plug in too quickly. Innovations always add some nutrition and open new doors, but basic knowledge, confidence, and motivation are prerequisites.

I find it ironic that AIGA education conferences lean toward emerging issues while there remains a well of naïveté about teaching the fundamentals. I think that this media-saturated generation needs to dirty its hands. Recognize that musical prodigies are likely to begin with the same fundamental scales and feisty lessons as did their ancestors. Roger Federer sweated the same forehand-backhand-volley drills as did Rod Laver fifty years earlier. For that matter, Federer still spends more hours practicing basic tennis strokes, that no one else has ever been better at, than he spends in games. That's one of the reasons why his matches finish quickly. It's not because of his high-tech equipment. Gutenberg's movable type of 1450 had a stupendous effect on the *quantity* of printed material but not necessarily a proportionate effect on its *quality*.

A related thought. Some of the assignments that I give, particularly to beginning students, look suspiciously like the ones I gave forty years ago. They may be classics, but the current students never had them—and I am not there to entertain myself but to educate a new generation. Incidentally, the lessons do evolve in nuanced ways and consequently continue to intrigue and teach me as well. New faculty often impatiently change for change's sake and may innocently think that an imagination gap prevents us old farts from doing so.

Assignments can be too complicated but never too simple.

I suggest that true creativity and project enthusiasm ideally comes from within rather than on the basis of a glamorous assignment and that creative potential is innate to every individual and to every phase of every project. For students, creative manifestations are more often realized by way of the perceptiveness and confidence that comes from thoughtfully focused exercises plus intuitive experimentation and one's interactions with same, rather than from brilliant lightbulb-like forethought. Woody Allen once said that "inspiration is for amateurs."

Certainly, we need to be inventively proactive in design education as the field develops, but, while some ingredients may be replaced, we should get more serious about extending studies. As a profession ferments, the need for specialization by way of advanced studies becomes necessary. So ultimately, digital design may be like anesthesiology, or information design like neurosurgery. Our education mindset may be formulated to move from general to focused studies and/or the reverse. I believe, however, that when one develops a depth of knowledge in some embraceable field, such as graphic design, one is then also better able to respect and/or to apply such wisdom to allied fields, and thus make other-discipline contributions. Generalization may then become a grounded career option. A knowledge base encourages radical freshness and complexity rather than trendy imitation or visual anarchy. Additionally, we should acknowledge that formal education is the beginning of a process. We must not get so confused by the complexities that we slight the first few steps in properly nudging a student's momentum. We must not be so broad that we confuse the beginner or suffocate the foundation, but we must not pigeonhole so narrowly that a graduate is only capable of repetitious stuttering.

Competence and awareness concerning graphic design education has certainly reverberated but while we have way too many schools offering such degrees, I fear that a majority still do not comprehend the principles behind the perspectives and approach that has been so successfully practiced at PCA/UA. Too often, assignments are shallow imitations without understanding conceptualization or the potential to engage visual form in a way that feeds critical thinking and communication along with aesthetic substance.

A fellow Ohio resident once said, "One small step for (a) man, one giant leap for mankind." So many teachers spend so much time concerned about their students' lack of liberal breadth, their naïveté, or the whatever elses that they fail to make their own small individual steps with each essential assignment. Our responsibility is not to complain about the things that our students do not know, but to teach. The process of investigating and designing a letterform can be as virtuous an educational undertaking as what is occurring across campus in some academic department. Elusive wisdom certainly relies, to some extent, on the variety of experiences, but equally on the depth of study.

Another related suggestion is that we stop feeling threatened by the emergence of amateur graphic design. Fifteen years ago at an AIGA event, I proposed that we should sanction **everyone** doing graphic design. Graphic design has to do with the use of a visual language, much like literature employs the written word. It should be seen as a fundamental humanist communications discipline rather than simply as a career path. We use visual design to document, express, report, incite, and inform. This is what journalists and creative writers do with words. We all write reports, diaries, letters, and sometimes even books and poetry. Our work doesn't denigrate the output of novelists and poets, nor does it really take jobs away from them. Quite the contrary: we appreciate their work and its peculiarities more because of our education in and experience with their tools, rules, and methods. If you play the game, you are more likely to envy the discipline and mastery of your idol, whether it is Tiger Woods or John Coltrane. This line of thought encourages my belief that we do not need certification in order to authenticate our professionalism, just as our world-class authors or musicians are not licensed . . . OK . . . Let's switch gears.

Some of the dumbest quasi-art I see is produced by **art** teachers themselves. Visual art education has become somewhat disingenuous compared with education in the hard and soft sciences or the performing arts. I might hypothesize that, while the artistic movement of abstract expressionism was a wonderful creative epiphany, it also helped to screw up public art education by seductively encouraging the replacement of discipline and skills in favor of a personal venting, while causing novices to try to squeeze out usually self-conscious new poop. This has splashed over into most college-level art programs as well. The result is a false artistry because the works are too often based on a spurious goal of just trying to be different, rather than for aesthetics and/or personal expression. This feeds into the public assumption that visual art is unteachable. I think that there is now more potency in the design fields than in the fine-art world and that designers are better equipped to lead the public education brigade. Frank Gehry's and Richard Sapper's works are sculpturally significant. Design should be a required subject in primary and secondary schools alongside of our word/sentence/language lessons. **We** should play a proactive role concerning inclusive visual literacy so that **every** Tom, Dick, and *Inge* can design materials at least as successfully as they author reports or letters to the editor.

Supposedly, the 1990s workplace buzzword "quality" has now been replaced with the word "design." Designers could aspire to marry the two terms for all levels of society.

One final topic is that there seems to be a growing romance with design research. That's great, because it adds weight to our entanglements and it feeds the robust authenticity of our field as a profession, but I suggest that an exaggerated worship of research, on its own, is perfunctory. The methodology and terminology concerning research can sound intimidating and it's easy to incorporate some enticing catchwords. As is the case with design practice, some research is grand but a lot of it is, at its core, mediocre. When subpar, it may reflect a simple hunting/ gathering, a revealing of the obvious, or self-gratification. Great designers and educators are the truly profound studs of our field. Theory is the more important and complex underpinning to design education and practice than are individualized support topics, such as research, history, criticism, or business. Different forms of research along with liberal and focused historical perspectives, plus critical analysis, all help to inform theory. However, the **doing** of **high design** is necessarily integral if any of it is to generate meaningful substance and enlightened manifestations. Incidentally, a dangerous mirage is materializing under the veil of "research" and, I fear, more because of financial pressures than may be acknowledged. I am referring to some colleges' adoration with grants and collaboratives. This can skewer an undergraduate educational mission and idealism in favor of a pimping for industry while competing with our alumni for some of the more attractive commissions.

What are some hopes for the future of graphic design education? I hope that the wave of political correctness is monitored. For instance, I read recently that there was some British move to replace, in schools, the designation of students' "failure" with the term "deferred success." I also wish that in the future, those individuals and organizations who habitually request free graphic design work from students and faculty will be required to do likewise for their health care, plumbing needs, legal counsel, and auto repairs. Also, that the people who claim to be professional but are responsible for the most glaring examples of visual swill in our environment will be forced to survive on an equally shallow diet of hot dog buns and cotton candy.

Contrary to what I said at the beginning, I am of course delighted and honored to be here today. I think of design as a regal profession, partially because, although some designers claim neutrality in their work in favor of each client's different needs, I believe that one's personal voice is inherent to every piece, while chronicling and contributing to our human legacy. This integral creative humanity is part of the magic of graphic design. To paraphrase Frank Lloyd Wright: "The designs that we produce are even more natural than a landscape because our works evolve from inspiration that has been translated through a human soul."

Thank you very much for staying with me and for what you do as designers, educators, or design groupies. Forty years ago, my wife Kathy was one of Inge Druckrey's and my first students. Our daughter Kelly has worked at some fine Philadelphia studios and is now a professor of graphic design at Michigan State University, while her sister Raegen is Nike's **most** creative apparel designer—so I hope that you all gain as much satisfaction from the design world as I have. Stay healthy by playing lots of tennis, even though your game pales next to Federer's—and **enjoy** today.

SUGGESTIONS

Lecture and presentation components (now enhanced with media advancements) are crucial, but best when interspersed with assignments and objective critiques. Since we are dealing verbally with visual communication,

a give-and-take between what is said and what is seen is most likely to bridge the translation gap. It makes sense to follow informational overtures with related exercises that encourage students to experiment with, visualize, and analyze the lesson content. An initial critique provides opportunities for additional information and understanding to be revealed by way of some respondent visuals. These group review sessions are essentially an extension of the lecture. Some critical information will not be understandable until a student has invested personal effort, has visual references, and is given a chance to digest each segment. We often need to see multiple iterations in order to absorb the particulars. Critiques should be thorough, informational, and motivational. It can be very beneficial for students to concurrently see others' responses and for the professor to be able to point out comparisons and differences by cross-referencing on a wall or a screen that is covered with examples.

It is helpful to build toward increased student participation by having them discuss each other's work. Beginning students are often reticent to comment on peer projects, but there are ways to initially facilitate this and nudge their ownership of the lessons. For instance, the person whose work was previously reviewed can initiate a critique for the subsequent student. Another quasi-gaming approach is to spin a bottle to determine who would lead off the commentary. These approaches help to somewhat playfully encourage student involvement while preventing the occasional grandstanders from dominating. Gradually, student adoption of the dialogue becomes increasingly contagious.

——

Students should be encouraged to redo their projects soon after a critique in order to best assimilate what was said about the visuals. There may be one, two, or several critiques prior to completion, depending on the assignment's breadth, but each is educational as nuances are peeled away. Students will realize that

the personal process of moving toward a resolution is a most important educational

component. This mindful and visual process
can be more revealing than the lectures or critiques. Each classroom assignment aims for just enough response variation to provide the fodder for a lesson, but if there is too much variation we may assume that the assignment was not clearly defined or it was too confusing.

——

When someone develops a depth of knowledge in an embraceable field, such as graphic design, he or she is then also able to respect and apply such wisdom to allied fields, and thus make other-discipline contributions. Accomplished designers have often stepped into related fields, much like a musician might navigate genres.

It is appropriate for beginning faculty to emulate the content they learned as students. This is not imitation unless it endures for decades without edification. It is better to use one's own experience—hopefully based on testing and some mature theory—rather than to artificially try to teach off of someone else's syllabus, unless it coincides with some very diligent mentoring. Reading about visual design or others' assignments cannot replicate a personal hands-on and thoughtful background, and it can be presumptive to invent an assignment if naively done as a whim to stoke one's independence. Gradually, faculty members build on their classroom encounters and, with evolving confidence, add insights that should elevate and expand course content.

—

Teachers need to prioritize what is best for the students rather than caressing their own professional agenda,

although the excitement that coincides with a particular faculty interest can inject a thrill and, when relevant to the lessons at hand, some meaningful content for the students. In lieu of that, it should not be difficult to find the intrigue in what may seem to be mundane. I might not be easily inspired to write a novel about my dumb desk. However, a professional author could have a tough time deciding whether to base a story on its manufacturing process, its materiality, the people who have touched it, speculating on its future users, its relationship to other objects, etc. An engaged design educator is never bored with a seemingly simple image or idea or a student's confusion, particularly given the group's diversity and the underlying project complexities. Beyond this, the sophistication and motivational efforts of the in-person educator's involvement is more impactful than the title of any given course or the content of its syllabus.

——

Lasagna Bolognese is a diner classic, blue jeans are iconic, and great novels continuously enrich. There are enduring classics in virtually every category of life. I suggest that there are similarly classic design/art assignments that provide superior educational opportunities without having an expiration date. Sometimes, as a result of trial and error plus thoughtfulness, the seemingly perfect exercise develops for a given stage of student development.

——

One cautionary note for us more mature dudes. We should be leery of pridefully inflating our generational history while complaining about how bad things are now. Our offspring are likely more knowledgeable and capable than we were. They face provocative new challenges and opportunities, will establish their own eloquent legacies, and will then reminisce about their good old days of the twenty-first century.

Any assignment that succinctly addresses certain needs or wishes and that releases some genuine understanding for students deserves continuation and evolution.

—

Such is the case with Josef Albers's *Interaction of Color* studies. In fact, my approach to form was inspired by Mr. Albers's attitude of visual experimentation and objective reading of what is seen. Similarly, my perspective favors the teachings of the Swiss designer and educator Armin Hofmann.

—

I encourage educators to develop their own palette of basic (from extremely simple and limited to more and more complex and ever more open-ended) exercises, where each challenge adds to and builds on the previous exercise so that a complexity of understanding gradually evolves. Basic exercises can ideally lead to usage and comprehension of my earlier described principles concerning harmony.

——

It is important to remember that the process, of thoughtfully experimenting and considering many alternative possibilities while looking carefully and *reading* the images, constitutes a learning-to-see-and-think encounter that is more important than the end product. Additionally, such **eyeball-anchored intensity stimulates one's intellectual acumen beyond the project at hand, because the pockets of our brain are intertwined.**

A trained designer may satisfy the client, but an educated designer can satisfy a larger audience as well as the client and him- or herself. In order to accomplish this, he or she should have a liberal perspective along with a focused comprehension of the opportunities, the obligations, and the tools of design.

MISCELLANY

5

FUNCTION

My text dwells primarily on how things look and on what
messages they transmit. This suggests an emphasis on the
field of graphic design (i.e., communication design, visual
communication) as opposed to an equal treatment for all
of the established design disciplines. Objects, materials,
and structures are, however, visual designs in addition to
their structural, environmental, and materials aspects. Their
two- and three-dimensional seen characteristics express
their purpose and personality, inform us, and should
contribute to their functional success and to the quality of
our environment. Buildings, tools, graphics, and clothing
share the visual language of color, shape, etc. Consequently,

I hope that there is a reasonable degree of discipline-universal relevance for this content. A primary goal of mine is to explain a commonsense perspective concerning design fundamentals and the successful, potentially thrilling employment of same.

———

Graphic design deals with the conceiving, planning, and production of aesthetically satisfying, socially responsible, expressive, and effective messages for communication.

———

This is primarily achieved through the sense of sight. It employs abstract form, symbolic imagery, and editorial text. The "graphic" term can be confusing because it traditionally implied a design-for-print notion. I suggest that, particularly in a contemporary context where electronic and other methods must be recognized, we may assume that it refers to the connotations of "directness" and "visual clarity."

———

It is not uncommon for this field to be mistakenly identified as "graphic arts" and for its purveyors to be referred to as "graphic artists." This is a misstep in that "graphic art" refers to reproduced work that is primarily done for the sake of expression and personal satisfaction (i.e., printmaking, silk screens, etchings, etc.) as opposed to work that responds to a communication issue and is done for public benefit.

———

I now suggest that **there are *four* fundamental graphic design project categories.** These are more generic than are our tools or particular formats (publications, digital, etc.). **This idea refers to what should be the dominant intent** in any project (primary purpose):

1.

PERSUASIVE | The primary intent is to motivate (compel) people to do something. The underlying concept often tends to be temporary or trendy in order to capitalize on contemporary thought or current events. Examples of this category include advertisements, political campaigns, social issue items, and consumer packaging.

2.

REPRESENTATIVE | (expressive, enhancive) The objective is to give a face to or to reveal the essence (mood) of the subject. The result may be either temporary or ongoing depending on the project. Examples of this category include corporate identification/branding, monetary items (currency, credit cards, postage stamps), games, greeting cards, and super-graphics.

We are paid by our clients but should remember that we are designing for the client's audience. Additionally, we are ethically obliged to consider all of the innocent bystanders who will be exposed to the results. We attempt to most directly connect with the proper audience while not imposing unnecessarily robust clutter for those bystanders. Always making an image big, bold, and red, or misappropriating some prepubescent catchword or shoddy image in order to grab attention equates with mindless gimmickry.

3

INFORMATIVE | The objective is to make information understandable, to educate, or to give directions. The result is often relatively long-lasting. Examples of this category include building and directional signs, maps, graphs, charts, menus, manuals, textbooks, calendars, and some digital applications.

4

EXPERIENTIAL | The designer conceives and/or establishes a plan of action, a system, or a program for dealing with some civic or organizational need. The result tends to play out over a period of time. This less-item-oriented design category will usually overlap one or more of the other three. There will often be an intersection of graphic with industrial design (technology/engineering) or another design field. Examples of this category include developing a business plan, managing a creative team, creating software, outlining an education curriculum, dealing with social or cultural issues, or strategizing for any organization. It may seem like a stretch to include this as an emerging graphic design specialty, since any visual obligation is likely peripheral or accomplished by others. However, since communication is central along with objective questioning, problem-solving acuity, an innate verve, a methodical mindset, and an advanced digital aptitude, professional graphic designers are appropriately positioned to serve in such a role. He/she is likely to function as a consultant for an established period of time or in a fixed capacity. The manifestations of such **design thinking** would probably, in fact, include visualized items such as graphs, hierarchical mapping, organization charts, or user interfaces.

—

Usually two or more of the preceding categories are incorporated, but it is helpful to avoid presumptions and to properly prioritize parallel categories. Indeed, many examples are not automatically exclusive to a particular category. For instance, designing a signing system for a zoo would necessitate differentiation within the system. We can assume that most of the signs are purely "informational" about the animals but that they should not aggressively impose themselves on the lush environment. They are, to an extent, initially "representative" in order to sensitively integrate with the natural surroundings, followed by the informational level of communication. However, the zoo signing for medical care or restrooms would need to be somewhat "persuasively" potent in relation to the information.

—

Words are vehicles, but astute typography transmits, translates, and inspires. A designer injects the content with some attitude and proper emphasis. In fact, despite what some preach, it is impossible for the designer to be absolutely neutral or anonymous. Each protagonist's voice will penetrate what is seen. However, this does not justify someone self-consciously inventing a personal style. Doing so will feel forced and be artificial. One's style will naturally reveal itself over a period of time.

Design success operates on different levels, but it initially intends to improve, solve, and/or to enlighten concerning the issue at hand. This explanation deviates from ideas that suggest "invention." As an example, it is not uncommon for someone to propose that a perfect example of industrial design is the paper clip. I disagree. The paper clip is a convenient invention, but it would be presumptuous for any industrial designer to claim its authorship for his/her field. There are many versions of paper clips, but only some are "designed" because people attempted to improve on the ease, usefulness, and appearance of a version of the concept category. Similarly, symbols or posters cannot be cited as excellent examples of "graphic design." They too are invention categories where success varies depending on the designed particulars.

———

Superior work is likely to be accomplished by the most curious and the most knowledgeable doers. **Excellent design solves societal problems in a creatively unexpected way that elevates the human spirit and influences beyond the particular context and time.**

———

Items (structures, ephemera, landscape, objects, clothing) are relatively temporary, but their impact is, to varying extents, ongoing. Every design discipline regularly requires collaboration with and the expertise of other personnel such as engineers and producers while contending with financial and schedule constraints. The objectives and the results are often positioned within a broad systems framework that may or may not have been conceived by the current participants.

———

Every design discipline shares the following portion of the graphic design definition (the conceiving, planning, and production of aesthetically satisfying, socially responsible, expressive, and effective . . .) but deviates in terms of the function component. All designers manipulate visual form, engage with similar problem-solving fundamentals, and must respect their allies' expertise in order to effectively work hand in hand. I believe that our knowledge and standards should be reflected in all of our selections and decisions. In relation to this, I question when any educated professional, who should aspire to excellence in his/her own field, demonstrates otherwise substandard values when it comes to other needs and indulgences. This is too

It is interesting that novices often try too hard to squeeze out an unusual idea. This is an artificial goal as opposed to just doing the job at hand. In fact, the most obvious concept is what will likely communicate most effectively to the greatest number of people. It can be surprisingly difficult to realize that what is staring us in the face may be the answer. The obvious often only seems to be so after it has been revealed. Rather than trying to force a concept, doing the most self-evident thing in an original way equates with legitimate creativity. The act of conception is satisfyingly dramatic but animalistic second nature and, ultimately, less meaningful than the nurturing that follows a birth.

often the case concerning art/design related choices. Also, we would expect that those organizations and merchants who clearly cherish quality in any one category deserve support and are likely to apply a universal concern for excellence.

———

On a side note, my dentist's office is attractive and comfortable, it provides current issues of various magazines in the waiting room, newish equipment, and they mostly stay on schedule. I think it is not coincidental that he is also an excellent dentist. I would be leery of a doctor or an attorney whose office is vapid or grungy. I feel that someone who professes excellence in any field portends a disingenuousness if enviable standards are otherwise dormant.

———

Particular design trends in any design field should not be downplayed as pure puffery. The particular styles that emerge are honest reverberations of and serve to document our current culture while refreshing our lives. A relevant fashion trend is likely to, in variously insidious ways, flow across all fields (design, art, politics, foods, government, literature, industry, and the entertainment categories).

———

All functional items have an appearance that is not restricted to gallery viewing. Their presence might as well be distinctive, even delicious, because the alternative is drabness or mimicry. Copying past accomplishments such as a style of design is a pedestrian exercise that, while avoiding risk, also repeats stereotypes, perpetuates knockoffs, and snuffs growth.

—

Appearance is not decorative frosting in design. Healthy aesthetics is a delight that feeds a human need and adds tasty digestibility. Since functional items ideally intend to improve on whatever they replace, their visual presence should also strive to elevate our existence and contribute to our legacy while occasionally invading the world of high artistry.

—

We should recognize that there is an important distinction between "design" and "decoration." **A designed item muscularly improves upon and intertwines function and form.** It manifests an "essence." A decorated item primarily toys with an item's cosmetic appearance, often to superficially change for change's sake or to fool us while offering empty calories. We would prefer that our friends

The communication effectiveness (functional) aspect of design is like the nutritional value of food while its formal (aesthetic) and emotional (expressive) qualities parallel food's taste, aroma, and presentation. It is not shallow to make a design appealing and digestible, thus causing mindful plus visceral reactions.

bathe as opposed to perfuming. For instance, most eyeglasses tend to be simplistic rehashes or self-consciously styled, while creatively "designed" versions are likely to strive for additional comfort, enhanced strength, better hinging, etc., as well as creating a handsome, lasting accessory that complements the wearer's presence. Excellent design may incorporate characteristics that mark a particular time period but it does so without tampering with an ongoing satisfaction and usefulness and is, therefore, timeless. Consider how mid-twentieth-century furniture classics often appear in and successfully complement the most cutting-edge architecture. Indeed, fine antiques also have lasting value in that they exhibit a love and craftsmanship that is not duplicated in a majority of new productions, including in those that mindlessly emulate the past. Additionally, I assert that there is a particular importance concerning the qualities of function-designed items in that they are necessary and omnipresent while we selectively choose when to visit a museum, order from a high-end menu, or attend a performance.

In design, **it is not necessary to sacrifice one objective for the others** (superior function, enticing form, or emotional engagement) but rather, the challenge is to have them mutually entwined. The result will then be an ongoing environmental version of poignant *and* savory nutrition.

—

It is important for any designer to avoid indifference or disrespect for his/her client's input. The client-team should be engaged as an accomplice to the problem-solving process because, along with the admission that they may sometimes be too close to the business at hand to be best able to objectively decipher some of the particulars, so too do they possess the most valuable internal expertise that must be successfully tapped. Ideally, the resulting design will generate a shared revelry by all parties.

Design is a subtractive as well as an additive process. The designer should, early on, question whether any accumulated rust needs to be cleaned away rather than foisting on the client a more costly replacement with something new. Classics often have quality and equity that never stales.

ABOUT**DESIGN**

AFTERWORD

In the five decades of Gordon Salchow's teaching and program leadership, the young field of graphic design was evolving and gradually defining itself as a mature design profession. Our educational institutions were equally formative. As Salchow's University of Cincinnati graphic design program grew through the second half of the twentieth century, the number of quality undergraduate graphic design programs in the US could be counted on one hand, possibly two. Today, literally hundreds of US schools offer a basically competent professional preparation to their undergraduate graphic design majors. This disciplinary progress and the health of today's graphic design education owe much to the leadership of the University of Cincinnati curriculum, a "philosophically grounded educational progression," in Salchow's words.

This book describes a lineage of four groundbreaking undergraduate programs: Minneapolis College of Art and Design (MCAD), Kansas City Art Institute (KCAI), Philadelphia College of Art, and the University of Cincinnati. This story also has much to do with the insights and influence of Rob Roy Kelly, a pioneering graphic design educator who is far less recognized than he should be. After receiving an MFA in graphic design at Yale University in 1955, Rob Roy Kelly began his innovative teaching at the Minneapolis College of Art and Design in 1957. As an MCAD undergraduate, Salchow made good use of his fortuitous study under Kelly. From 1964 through 1974, a sympathetic Kansas City Art Institute president gave Rob Roy Kelly the opportunity to fully develop his educational vision in his KCAI graphic design department. There, Gordon Salchow cut his teeth as a new teacher after also attending Yale's MFA graphic design program, at Kelly's encouragement. At KCAI, Salchow was part of Kelly's close-knit faculty, which included the first two Kunstgewerbeschule Basel–trained graphic design educators to teach in the US, Inge Druckrey and Hans Allemann, at the inception of the very important Swiss influence in American graphic design education and practice.

The Kansas City Art Institute period was brief. The visas of Druckrey and Alleman, the two Basel-educated teachers, required their return to Europe. In the early 1970s, both joined the faculty at Philadelphia College of Art under the direction of Ken Hiebert and became key long-term faculty in that rigorous Swiss-influenced program. In 1968, Salchow left KCAI to build his own graphic design program at the University of Cincinnati, again at the encouragement of

Rob Roy Kelly. At Cincinnati, Salchow notes that he "incorporated some of the Basel qualities" that he absorbed from his KCAI Swiss-trained colleagues. The long-lived Cincinnati and Philadelphia design programs have marked a sharp turn away from American graphic design's earlier manifestations in book typography, commercial art, and advertising design, and played an important role in the professionalization of graphic design in the US.

———

Salchow noted the personal impact of the KCAI experience in a 2004 interview: "I know that my own enthusiasm for the profession and for design education, my fundamental sense of professional ethics, and a personal confidence were greatly inspired by working with Rob. Also, prior to my intimate working relationships with Inge and Hans, my own design work was clean but stiff; it simplistically attended to selection and organization rather than including form-making, lacked any real experimental edge or personality, and was product- rather than process-driven." In fact, in the 1960s, form, experiment, and process were generally absent in American graphic design. In his years as an educator and designer, Salchow has made form, experiment, and process key elements.

———

At Cincinnati, Salchow rejected the frequent art school contention that "visual art is unteachable," as he characterizes it. Because graphic design education originated in university art departments and independent art colleges, our discipline grew out of a "commercial" application of fine arts beliefs. This has led to a traditional assumption that the practice of graphic design rests on the intuitive genius of the individual artist/designer, the brilliant creator; and that design education's purpose is to spur the expression of the student's inner creativity. This could be described as the "aha!" or "big idea" school of graphic design education, the dominant educational paradigm in the US when Salchow began teaching. This older approach relies on the students' emulation of revered designers and illustrators, who typically teach part-time as a complement to their own professional practice. These part-time faculty, however distinguished they might be, are often unaware of their course's relationship to the program's other course offerings and rarely interact with fellow faculty to create a comprehensive curricular vision and course sequence.

Instead, Salchow began his program at University of Cincinnati in 1968 by engaging well-educated, full-time educators who also practiced design—the reverse of the earlier "commercial art" approach. He applied the lessons of Rob Roy Kelly and his Swiss colleagues at KCAI to initiate a systematic and comprehensive menu of sequential courses with projects calibrated to create a curriculum that **teaches**. Students learned repeatable processes, assimilating and consistently applying the conceptual scope, visual craft, and joy of our discipline—in Salchow's words, "teachably objective principles that facilitate one's problem-solving and creative capabilities." This educational model relies on the master teacher rather than the design master.

The central goal of those earlier schools' intuitive, personality-based, and unstructured "commercial art" education—and regrettably of a percentage of current curricula—is to secure a graduate's first job. Salchow envisions design education as far more, a "fundamental humanist communications discipline rather than simply as a career path." Yet through the years, University of Cincinnati graduates have been impressively successful in securing those great first jobs, and more importantly, many have matured into design leaders.

The synthesis of Kelly's vision, Swiss methods, and Salchow's innovative curriculum stresses a fundamental sensitivity and critical eye to design's aesthetic visual elements. But in today's rapid-fire communication media soup involving motion, sound, time, and digital code, many question the relevance of visual fundamentals—design forms, aesthetics, harmony, and perfection. Salchow contends that these fundamentals should be seen as an essential "visualized investigation . . . seemingly simple assignments revealed and caused complexities of thought and understanding" applicable to all communication media.

Unfortunately many graphic design educators view design aesthetics and design functionality as mutually exclusive realms. As a result, design curricula are frequently organized around one or the other. The aesthetic side focuses on visual refinement in compositional form and typography, while the functionalists stress research, theory, and methodology. Under Salchow, the University of Cincinnati curriculum found a productive balance, with distinctively rigorous visual training complemented by pragmatic problem-solving methods. The connection between form and function are furthered by the University of Cincinnati's unique internship schedule in which a semester of paid co-op work alternates with each semester of course study.

In spite of his emphasis on the visual, it's notable that in this book Salchow has intentionally included far fewer images and illustrations than the usual design treatise. The typical book on graphic design relies heavily on illustrations, and many images would be expected in a book dealing with the visual phenomena of point, line, shape, space, color, and harmony. One could wonder why Salchow has not made use of the abundance of superb student design work from his years of project assignments focusing on these visual elements.

Salchow's stated goal is to "inspire perpetually individualized visual investigations." The absence of images here helps make the case that these visual essentials transcend any particular style and are equally applicable to all formal vocabularies. This can be an effective strategy that avoids attaching a stylistic bias to Salchow's visual essentials, in the hope that readers will find their own visual expressions of these essentials of graphic form.

This is important because graphic design is a practice characterized (and plagued) by a historic cavalcade of styles often sampled by students and young designers as a stylistic banquet on which to feast. On the other hand, our early modernist heritage continues to create significant "design guilt" over the use of graphic style and eclecticism. Designers perpetually debate the validity of style and the possibility of universal form, free of associations with specific cultures and historical periods. Salchow's own design portfolio is rooted firmly in what some would generalize as "Swiss style," or the visual vocabulary of abstracted geometricized minimalism rooted in the Bauhaus ideal of universal form and the Swiss school's visual methods. Much of Salchow's personal form and that of his students has carried these stylistic markers of the mid-century modernist Swiss school, so examples of Cincinnati student work could attach a stylistic vocabulary to the visual essentials.

But it should be noted that Salchow's personal graphic design expression has morphed through the years, while retaining a distinctive mastery of these visual essentials. For instance, Salchow's inventive design work in the mid-1970s broke cherished modernist rules and expanded graphic design's visual possibilities, even as his keen sense of visual dynamics continued to guide his work.

In addition, this book's minimal use of images demonstrates the axiom that a narrower communication bandwidth demands and stimulates more active and engaged readers, as they construct their own visualizations of Salchow's written words. Salchow compares this to the power of radio's narrow bandwidth, "much like I fantasized the world when enthralled by radio dramas in my youth."

Salchow employs frequent athletic comparisons to advocate the designer's aspiration to an elevated visual proficiency and level of control, refined by years of close looking, self-discipline, practice, and focused critique. He contends that visual acuity is "as complex but also as teachable as is driving, piano playing, or soccer," and that "education and practice greatly enhance one's abilities and the credibility of our judgment." He feels the graphic designer's expertise can eventually become spontaneous "without conscious thought after it becomes second nature" through much disciplined practice on fundamentals.

—

This focus on visual fundamentals resonates with my experience. As my years of teaching have proceeded, I find that basic design principles, while critical for young students new to design, are even more resonant for experienced designers. At my vantage point of fifty years of design practice and teaching, these principles are ever more comprehensible. Salchow's fundamentals place all those things we know well from experience into a meaningful framework. In his view, visual fundamentals order the visual physical world and also embody larger meaning.

—

Perhaps the basic design exercises in Salchow's disciplined training regimen might better be assigned at the end of a course of study, rather than at the beginning; or perhaps repeated in students' final assignments (an impractical proposal, of course). In my own undergraduate experience, when a second design major required me to repeat these basic exercises, I was more able to grasp the purpose of the basic design "point-line-plane" assignments and execute them far better as an advanced student than as a freshman.

—

Projects focused on Salchow's tenets would be even more gratifying to execute now, at this farther point of my personal design trajectory. Perhaps there should be a design program for the senior designer, dedicated to the great pleasure of giving form to basic design projects. Some sublime graphic form would surely be the result. Self-initiated examples are seen in the current personal work of venerable designers, including Willi Kunz's new book *Phantasmagorias: Daydreaming with Lines* and Burton Kramer's color composition paintings of "music made visual."

This book's focus on long-term teaching practice demonstrates a master educator's growth. Educators' insights are the outcome of years of critical thought and teacherly iterations. It is a sad mistake to cast one's courses in concrete. A nationally awarded high school educator once remarked that teachers should know they are in trouble when they laminate their lesson plans and assignments, preserving them for use year after year. Teaching a course repeatedly is a valuable opportunity to iterate. Every course assignment can be a laboratory experiment in which to test a new variable. Student outcomes demonstrate the usefulness (or not!) of that new assignment variable. Iteration enables assignments to evolve, address new conditions, and break new ground.

Salchow is evidence that, although education is ostensibly about students' learning, the educator learns the most. Effective teachers know one cannot rely on simple authority to encourage a students' work forward with just "because I say so." Instead, engaged teachers are continually challenging themselves to go beyond personal opinion and base their reasoning on a developing conceptual framework and disciplinary vision—a lifelong learning process. Salchow attributes much personal growth to his "constructively feisty and astute colleagues" at the University of Cincinnati and his student interactions.

Salchow's athletic comparisons of practice, precision, and discipline run through this book. The sports coach shares something with the educator. In many ways, teaching is like coaching. And the lessons of athletics are important to Salchow's personal story. He credits his tennis athleticism as a key to his adult persona; his daughter Kelly (named for Salchow's mentor, Rob Roy Kelly) is an Olympic rowing athlete as well as a graphic design educator; and his daughter Raegen has been a Nike athletic apparel designer for a number of years.

The Salchow family name brings another athletic metaphor to mind. It's notable that the "Salchow" is a key figure skating jump invented by the Swedish ice skater Ulrich Salchow in 1909. This jump literally embodies and physicalizes a potent design concept. Before the gravity-defying Salchow jump, the figure skater increases speed and executes a quick precise turn from front to back, followed by an all-important "check"—a momentary pause that stops the body's rotation before the powerful leg swing and spring into the jump. The perfection of this sequence significantly increases the speed, height, and distance of the skater's dramatic leap into the air. Salchow's calibrated thoughts on visual precision parallel the Salchow jump's method. Even the most muscular or intuitively gifted designers benefit from the quick turn to the back and the precise pause—a disciplined review of the essentials, "checking" intuition with critical consideration and experiential depth—before taking the dynamic leap forward into a unique expression of visual communication. Through rigorous practice, this movement becomes deeply internalized, enabling fluid execution for both skaters and designers.

In the physics of ice skating, perfect form yields maximum power. Perhaps the same holds true for graphic design, pointing to the relationship of form and function. Form can go beyond style to create a powerful resonance with the audience. Form not only enhances function, form can be function.

Katherine McCoy

AUTHOR

Gordon Salchow is a Professor Emeritus at the University of Cincinnati where he was appointed, in 1967, to develop a new curriculum and a department of graphic design. Its initiatives and its success quickly established UC as one of graphic design's most respected educational institutions. He directed this academic unit for many years, continuing in a full-time teaching role, and then retired in 2010. Previous to Cincinnati, Professor Salchow taught at the Kansas City Art Institute. He has a Master of Fine Arts degree from Yale University and a Bachelor of Fine Arts degree from the Minneapolis College of Art and Design.

Salchow has been a guest lecturer for various organizations, conferences, and universities. His design work and articles have appeared in numerous exhibitions, periodicals, and books. He has often judged competitions, and he served on more than a dozen National Endowment for the Arts Design Improvement Program panels from 1974 to 1985; chaired the Ohio Arts Council's Design Arts Advisory Panel in 1982 and 1983; and has participated on a variety of other professional panels. Salchow was Vice President of Education for the American Institute of Graphic Arts while serving on its National Board of Directors (1988–1993), and in 2007 the AIGA honored him, along with Noel Martin, as Cincinnati's first National AIGA Fellows. Additionally, he was the 1992 recipient of the Cincinnati Art Directors' Club's Lifetime Achievement Award and the 1985 recipient of the Minnesota Graphic Design Association's similar Design for Society Award.

The author hopes that this book will provide some clarity, challenge a few assumptions, and helpfully contribute to our ongoing dialogue concerning art and design.

INDEX

⌐ABOUT⌐**DESIGN**

⌐ABOUT⌐DESIGN

BOOKS FROM ALLWORTH PRESS

ADVERTISING DESIGN AND TYPOGRAPHY
by Alex W. White (8.5 x 11, 224 pages, paperback, $29.99)

BECOMING A DESIGN ENTREPRENEUR
by Steven Heller and Lita Talarico (6 x 9, 208 pages, paperback, $19.99)

BRAND THINKING AND OTHER NOBLE PURSUITS
by Debbie Millman with Rob Walker (6 x 9, 336 pages, paperback, $19.95)

CITIZEN DESIGNER (SECOND EDITION)
by Steven Heller and Véronique Vienne (6 x 9, 272 pages, paperback, $22.99)

DESIGN FIRMS OPEN FOR BUSINESS
by Steven Heller and Lita Talarico (7.5 x 9.25, 256 pages, paperback, $24.95)

DESIGN LITERACY
by Steven Heller with Rick Poynor (6 x 9, 304 pages, paperback, $22.50)

DESIGN THINKING
by Thomas Lockwood (6 x 9, 304 pages, paperback, $24.95)

DESIGNERS DON'T READ
by Austin Howe with Fredrik Averin (5.5 x 8.5, 224 pages, paperback, $19.95)

THE EDUCATION OF A GRAPHIC DESIGNER
by Steven Heller (6 x 9, 380 pages, paperback, $19.99)

THE ELEMENTS OF GRAPHIC DESIGN
by Alex W. White (8 x 10, 224 pages, paperback, $29.95)

GRAPHIC DESIGN RANTS & RAVES
by Steven Heller (7 x 9, 200 pages, paperback, $19.99)

To see our complete catalog or to order online, please visit www.allworth.com.